Public Talk Series: 5

VALUE OF VALUES

The Pointer out the door

SWAMI DAYANANDA SARASWATI
ARSHA VIDYA

Arsha Vidya
Research and Publication Trust
Chennai

Published by :
Arsha Vidya Research and Publication Trust
4 ' Sri Nidhi ' Apts 3rd Floor
Sir Desika Road Mylapore
Chennai 600 004 INDIA
Tel : 044 2499 7131, 2499 7023
Email : avrandpt@gmail.com
Website : www.avrpt.com

ISBN : 978 - 81 - 903636 - 7 - 9

Upto 8th Reprint 15,000 Copies
9th Reprint : July 2017 Copies : 1000

Design & Layout:
Graaphic Design

Printed at :
Sudarsan Graphics Pvt. Ltd.,
27, Neelakanta Mehta Street
T. Nagar, Chennai 600 017
Email : info@sudarsan.com

Contents

	Preface	v
	Key to Transliteration	vi
	Values and Vedanta	1
	Universal Values: Source and Function	9
	Twenty Values of an Enlightened Mind	31
1	Absence of Conceit – *Amānitvam*	35
2	Absence of Pretence – *Adambhitvam*	47
3	Not hurting – *Ahiṁsā*	53
4	Glad Acceptance – *Kṣāntiḥ*	60
5	Straightforwardness – *Ārjavam*	68
6	Service to the Teacher – *Ācāryopāsanam*	70
7	Inner and Outer Purity – *Śaucam*	74
8	Steadfastness – *Sthairyam*	88
9	Mastery Over the Mind – *Ātmavinigrahaḥ*	90
10	Dispassion toward Sense Objects – *Indriyārtheṣu Vairāgyam*	95

11	Absence of Self-importance – *Anahaṅkāraḥ*	102
12	Reflection on the Limitations of Birth, Death, Oldage, Sickness and Pain – *Janma-mṛtyu-jarā-vyādhi-duḥkha-doṣānudarśanam*	107
13	Absence of a Sense of Ownership – *Asaktiḥ*	112
14	Absence of Obsession toward Son, Wife, House and so on – *Anabhiṣvangaḥ Putra-dāra-gṛhādiṣu*	121
15	Constant Equanimity... *Nityaṁ Samacittatvam...*	123
16	Unswerving Devotion to Me, the Lord – *Mayi Ananya-yogena Bhaktiḥ Avyabhicāriṇī*	129
17	Preference for a Secluded Place – *Vivikta-deśa-sevitvam*	136
18	Absence of Craving for Social Interaction – *Aratiḥ Jana-saṁsadi*	140
19	Commitment to Self-knowledge – *Tattva-jñānārtha-darśanam*	144
20	Understanding the Ultimate Validity of Self-knowledge – *Adhyātma-jñāna-nityatvam*	152
	Values: Preparation For Listening, Reflection and Contemplation	179

Preface

A value like ahiṁsā is universal. It is so because every human being through his or her common sense knows it. Preaching a value, therefore, has no value. But each value is to be assimilated so that it does not get compromised under pressure of greed, pride, infatuation and so on.

This book initiates the process of assimilation of certain important values and healthy attitudes discussed in the Bhagavad Gītā. A well-assimilated value becomes part of oneself like even the value of hygiene. Deliberate living of a chosen value is a must to complete the process of assimilation. May this book help the reader grow into one totally acceptable to oneself.

Swami Dayananda Saraswati
Rishikesh
19 March 2007

Key to Transliteration and Pronunciation of Sanskrit Letters

Sanskrit is a highly phonetic language and hence accuracy in articulation of the letters is important. For those unfamiliar with the Devanāgari script, the international transliteration is a guide to the proper pronunciation of Sanskrit letters.

अ	*a*	*(but)*	ट	*ṭa*	*(true)**3
आ	*ā*	*(father)*	ठ	*ṭha*	*(anthill)**3
इ	*i*	*(it)*	ड	*ḍa*	*(drum)**3
ई	*ī*	*(beat)*	ढ	*ḍha*	*(godhead)**3
उ	*u*	*(full)*	ण	*ṇa*	*(under)**3
ऊ	*ū*	*(pool)*	त	*ta*	*(path)**4
ऋ	*ṛ*	*(rhythm)*	थ	*tha*	*(thunder)**4
ॠ	*ṝ*	*(marine)*	द	*da*	*(that)**4
ऌ	*ḷ*	*(revelry)*	ध	*dha*	*(breathe)**4
ए	*e*	*(play)*	न	*na*	*(nut)**4
ऐ	*ai*	*(aisle)*	प	*pa*	*(put)* 5
ओ	*o*	*(go)*	फ	*pha*	*(loophole)**5
औ	*au*	*(loud)*	ब	*ba*	*(bin)* 5
क	*ka*	*(seek)* 1	भ	*bha*	*(abhor)**5
ख	*kha*	*(blockhead)**1	म	*ma*	*(much)* 5
ग	*ga*	*(get)* 1	य	*ya*	*(loyal)*
घ	*gha*	*(log hut)**1	र	*ra*	*(red)*
ङ	ṅa	*(sing)* 1	ल	*la*	*(luck)*
च	*ca*	*(chunk)* 2	व	*va*	*(vase)*
छ	*cha*	*(catch him)**2	श	*śa*	*(sure)*
ज	*ja*	*(jump)* 2	ष	*ṣa*	*(shun)*
झ	*jha*	*(hedgehog)**2	स	*sa*	*(so)*
ञ	*ña*	*(bunch)* 2	ह	*ha*	*(hum)*

ं	*ṁ*	*anusvāra*	(nasalisation of preceding vowel)
ः	*ḥ*	*visarga*	(aspiration of preceding vowel)
*			No exact English equivalents for these letters

1.	Guttural	–	Pronounced from throat
2.	Palatal	–	Pronounced from palate
3.	Lingual	–	Pronounced from cerebrum
4.	Dental	–	Pronounced from teeth
5.	Labial	–	Pronounced from lips

The 5th letter of each of the above class – called nasals – are also pronounced nasally.

Values and Vedanta

In Chapter xiii of the Bhagavad Gītā, there are a few verses that deal with what we may call 'values'. The *Gītā* calls these values *jñāna,* which means knowledge. However, *jñāna,* used in the sense of values, is not the knowledge of the self that is both the means and the end of Vedantic teaching. Here, *jñāna* stands for the collection of qualities of the mind in the presence of which, in a relative measure, knowledge of the self can take place; in the substantial absence of which, self-knowledge does not take place, no matter how adequate is the teacher or how authentic is the teaching.

Knowledge requires three factors

Three factors are required for knowledge to take place. These are the knower, the object of knowledge and the means of knowledge. These three factors must be present for any knowledge to take place. Our everyday experiences demonstrate the importance of these factors. Take, for example, the knowledge of sound. Firstly, we need the knower, the subject, to hear the sound. Secondly, the sound that has to be known or heard should be there. Finally, we need the means, the ears that are capable of hearing.

These are straightforward factors, except the third factor, which may require some analysis. Factor number one presents no problems; it is clear to me that if I am not there within the range of the sound, I will not hear it. Factor number two also is self-evident; if the sound does not occur, I will not hear it. Factor number three may not be that simple. Let us say that according to reliable reports, a sound did occur and I was within the range of the sound. Nonetheless, I did not hear the sound. All that it means is that I have to check the capability of my ears, which are the means of knowledge for sound.

Mind must back sense organs

If acoustical tests show that my ears are capable of hearing, but I did not hear the sound, the problem must lie elsewhere. Perhaps, I was not attentive; my attention wandered. What does it mean? It means that my mind was not attentively backing my ears. I was there; the sound occurred; my ears were there and were capable; but my mind was not behind my ears to light them up for listening. Therefore, I must add something to my understanding of what constitutes an adequate means of knowledge. An adequate means of knowledge must include the appropriate and capable sense organ—eyes for vision, ears for sound, tongue for taste, nose for smell and skin for touch. In addition, there must be an attentive, capable mind behind the sense organ. From this we understand that for simple perceptual knowledge, the sense organs alone are not the *pramāṇa*, the means of knowledge; the sense organs along with the mind are the *pramāṇa*. When all factors including the mind are present, knowledge takes place.

Mind must be prepared

When all factors, including an attentive mind, are present does knowledge always take place? What if I am seeking the knowledge of calculus? I find a competent professor of calculus, who is a good teacher, with the ability to communicate what he knows. He teaches me in English, a language I know. I recognise the words. To illustrate, he writes numbers and letters on the blackboard. I know and can identify the numbers and letters.

I am physically able to see what he writes on the board. I sincerely wish to learn calculus. I regularly attend the classes. The professor teaches while I listen and look. My mind is behind my ears and my eyes. Yet, calculus knowledge does not come to me. Why? My mathematics background is shaky; I am not certain whether 7 plus 4 equals 9 or 12! It means that I lack the necessary preparation for calculus.

It is obvious that we must add something more to our understanding of an adequate means of knowledge. We saw that a means of knowledge must be appropriate, capable, and backed by an attentive mind. Now, we must add yet another qualification. The mind, at least in some instances, must not only be capable and attentive but also be prepared. In order to be ready for calculus knowledge, a *saṁskāra,* a certain discipline in mathematics is required. Only then can we get calculus knowledge.

Words as a means of knowledge

For simple perceptual knowledge, no particular preparation may be necessary other than, perhaps, calling the mind to attention. When an object is there, the eyes are open and the mind is behind the eyes, the object is seen, then we obtain visual knowledge of that object, without any special preparation. However, for knowledge such as calculus, which is more than mere perceptual knowledge, some preparation is always necessary. Further, for words to work as a valid means of knowledge the teacher must wield them properly and the student's mind must be ready.

Vedanta is a *pramāṇa,* a means of knowledge in the form of words and sentences. When a competent teacher wields them, they must reveal the truth of the self. Words give direct or indirect knowledge depending on the object involved. If the object is within my range of experience, words can bring about direct knowledge. Vedanta is about me, the first person singular 'I'. I am always available to myself; therefore, words can give me direct knowledge about myself.

If the words are to convey knowledge, the student must understand the words exactly in the same sense as understood by the teacher who wields them. The teacher here is the one who uses the words to impart the vision of the subject taught. General definitions are not sufficient. Inherent to their generality, they are prone to subjective interpretations. For words to serve as *pramāṇa*, their precise intended meaning must be conveyed; the unintended possible meanings must be negated. How does a teacher accomplish this? He establishes a context in which the other possible meanings of the words are ruled out. When a teacher fails to create a context for the words he uses, he cannot convey knowledge through them. Then, words only become another form of conditioning. This commonly happens when the subject matter is the self. Frequently, in a teaching attempting to reveal the self, words such as 'infinite', 'Brahman', 'eternal' are used but not unfolded. Such words only create a new conditioning, thereby adding to the confusion and vagueness in the mind of the student. However, even when you have both a qualified teacher of Vedanta, learned in the methodology of teaching, who knows how to unfold the precise meaning of the words used, and a dedicated student who is seeking knowledge of the self, the knowledge that is Vedanta cannot take place unless the student's mind is prepared. For a student with an unprepared mind, Vedanta becomes like calculus for a person still working on his multiplication tables. This does not mean that calculus or Vedanta cannot be understood. It simply means that preparation of the mind is required. The *antaḥkaraṇa,* the mind, is the place where knowledge takes place. If knowledge does not take place when both the object of knowledge and an appropriate means of knowledge are available to the person who wants the knowledge, then there must be some obstacle that is responsible for preventing the knowledge taking place. The obstacle is a lack of preparation of the mind.

'JÑĀNA' PREPARES THE MIND FOR VEDANTA

What prepares the mind for the knowledge of Vedanta? Practice such as *prāṇāyāma,* certain breathing exercises and *āsanas,* certain postures, may be useful in quietening a restless mind but they do not prepare the mind for self-knowledge. *Jñāna,* according to the *Gītā,* prepares the mind for Vedanta. *Jñāna* can be defined as a state of mind that reflects certain universal values and ethical attitudes. Other practices may bring about a mental quietude in which the necessary values are more readily established, but only discovery and assimilation of the values help to prepare the mind. Therefore, the *Gītā* raises the appropriate values to the status of '*jñāna*', a word that means knowledge. However, the '*jñāna* - values' and '*jñāna* - self-knowledge' must not be confused. They are not the same thing. The '*jñāna*' of values is preparation for the gaining of self-knowledge. It is not that when the mind enjoys the appropriate values, knowledge of the self necessarily occurs, but that without appropriate values it cannot occur. We can enlist three positions. One is when the appropriate values are present, but self-knowledge may or may not be present. The second is when the appropriate values are present, and self-knowledge can be gained. The third is when appropriate values are absent and self-knowledge cannot be gained.

Universal Values: Source and Function

What is a value? 'Value' indicates the regard for a thing, situation, or attitude, which for some reason is esteemed or prized by the value holder. The appropriate values, which prepare the mind for Vedanta, are certain universal ethical attitudes. In Sanskrit an ethical value can be defined as *dharma*. *Dharma* is a standard or norm of conduct derived from the way in which I wish others to view or treat me. The 'dharmic' mandates for behaviour and attitude, though commonly found in religious scriptures, in fact, trace their source to pragmatic common sense ethics, which religious ethics confirm. In other words, my norm for what is 'proper' behaviour or a 'good' attitude is based on the way I wish others to treat or view me. What I expect or want from others becomes my standard for *dharma*, right behaviour; what I do not want others to do is *adharma*, wrong behaviour. I want others to speak truth to me. I do not want others to lie to me. Speaking the truth is *dharma* for me. Speaking the non-truth is *adharma* for me. Scriptures confirm speaking truth as good behaviour and speaking non-truth as bad behaviour.

Other behaviour norms such as non-hurting, humility, charity, are all based upon the same consideration of how I would like others to treat me. Thus, ethical norms are not just arbitrary man-made rules but stem from an inherent, common regard for one's own interest and comfort. Ethical standards are natural and universal. There may be some cultural variations in degree or emphasis but the basic standards have certain universality.

ETHICAL VALUES: UNIVERSAL IN CONTENT AND RELATIVE IN APPLICATION

The universality of acceptable codes of conduct, that is, of general ethical standards, does not mean that these standards are absolute. *Dharma* and *adharma* are both relative. There are situations where what is considered ethical in one situation, becomes unethical in another, depending on the context. That a standard may be relative does not mean that it is purely subjective. Although relative, sometimes in applicability, basic ethical standards have a universal content. There is a similarity in everyone's reaction to being hurt, cheated, lied to and bullied. Ethical standards are based on human consensus regarding what is the acceptable conduct; this consensus is not negated by the fact that the norms may be subject to interpretation in some situations. Even such a pronounced clear value as non-hurting to myself is modified by circumstance when I willingly submit to the surgeon's knife. Such a suspension of my value for non-injury to myself is situational and does not affect my basic value for non-injury to me or to it's extension, that is my general value for non-hurting to all beings.

Although my norms or values for behaviour and attitudes themselves may not be subjective, my interpretation of these values is very likely to be subjective. My values are universal in content but relative and situational in my application of them. For example, I am likely to apply a value for truthfulness very consistently and absolutely to the words of others; to my own words my application will be much less consistent and quite relative to the situation.

In general practice, I will apply values more consistently and more absolutely to others than to myself. After all, the source of my values is found in the way in which I want others to treat me which becomes my norm for 'good' behaviour. I find it easy to have others observe ethical standards, so I can be the beneficiary. It seems less easy for me to be consistent in the application of these standards to my own behaviour.

Ethical values cannot be dismissed

Can I safely dismiss a concern for values? No, I cannot escape from values. No one living in this world can escape relationships, based upon his concern that he may not be hurt or disturbed. From this comes an accepted canon in the criminal code, 'do not be an informer'. The example of a 'hit man' reveals the inescapability of the impact of values. A veteran 'hit man', a merciless killer, does not want himself to be 'hit'. He cannot escape the value for not hurting; he can only defy it, which creates conflicts even in a de-sensitised mind. Values cannot be dismissed, nor can they be defied with impunity. Failure to meet a value puts me in conflict with myself. When I perform an action that is a non-value for me, I create a seed of guilt, which is all that is needed to produce sleeplessness, fear and conflict. Even small lies create problems, like lying our age. It may seem a simple, unimportant thing, but small lies register inside as conflicts.

ARE VALUES ONLY MITHYĀ, APPARENT?

Those who have had a little exposure to the teaching of Vedanta, may believe that norm-breaking behaviour, that is, adharmic behaviour may be dismissed because it is only '*mithyā*', apparent, and not absolutely real. To such an argument, it can be said: If you can dismiss all dharmic acts also as *mithyā,* apparent, then certainly you may dismiss bad acts as well. When you can see good and bad equally as *mithyā,* values are not a problem for you. In the clear knowledge of what is real and what is apparent, your actions in the relative world cannot but be spontaneously good, because you have nothing to gain, nothing to protect. It is that clear knowledge of the self, which you are seeking. To be ready to discover that knowledge, your mind must be prepared with proper values. In a mind filled with conflicts, because values are dismissed or defied, knowledge will not take place when you listen to the teacher of Vedanta.

Values and conflict

No one wants a mind in conflict. A mind in conflict is not a desirable mind. Once conflicts are there, problems of the mind are unavoidable. Self-condemnation, regret, guilt, and a sense of failure are the products of a mental conflict. Conflicts come when I am unable to live up to a particular value which, consciously or unconsciously, I accept. Societal norms have a universal content, the influence of which I cannot really escape. My inherent desire to be comfortable and secure compels me to set standards for others' behaviour, establishing a common sense ethical code which bounces back. Religion codifying society's ethical consensus into a rigid table of do's and don'ts, make non-conformity on my part even more difficult. When I cannot live up to my value structure, I am in conflict and suffer guilt.

'Dropping-out' does not solve conflict

The 'drop-out' behaviour of the 'hippie generation' prevalent during the 60's in the West, largely seems to have been an attempt to escape conflicts. During the Vietnam War period, the clash of unassimilated traditional values with situational personal values was particularly acute for young people. The response of many was an attempt to make 'no values' their basic value. Traditional values were condemned and a life-style based on 'individuality', 'self-expression' and 'spontaneity' was proclaimed in their stead. This did not work. True, values led to conflict; but, as we saw before, values cannot simply be dropped. The universal content of values can be negated only if I have no concern how the other person treats me. If I want other people to behave in a certain manner, I am caught in a value system.

How values cause conflict

When I have a value structure that I follow and expect others to follow in the same manner, my values cause me no conflict. However, when I want others to behave in a certain way, but for my own reasons, I am not able or willing to behave in that way, I have a problem. When I have a value and something interferes with my expression of that value, I am in conflict with myself. What interferes with my expression of my general values? Individual situational values, linked with some highly desired personal end, can interfere with my expression of general values, when the general values have not become fully assimilated personal values for me.

The universal value for truth provides a good example of a general standard which, frequently, is only half assimilated. Let us look at the value of speaking the truth. I want everyone to speak the truth to me. It is a universal value. I am also obliged to speak the truth by the various authorities. My parents command or advise me to speak the truth. Society and religion asks me to speak the truth. Speaking truth is a part of my value system.

When it comes to assimilating this value with reference to others, the value of others' truthfulness is immediately clear to me. I am aware that when someone gives me false information, it is inconvenient and or harmful to me. My value for others' truthfulness to me is both personal and well-assimilated.

With reference to myself, the value of my being truthful is not immediately clear to me. I do not see what I get out of being truthful. However, I am aware that I am obliged to speak the truth.

It obliges my parents, my society and my religious code.

The disconnection between what I expect of others and what I do results in my having a split value, one half is personal while the other is obligatory. The value for money illustrates the development and assimilation of a powerful, personal situational value.

Value for money

When I was a child of three, I once picked up a piece of paper. It was a piece of green paper[1] printed, and colourful. I began, as I did with every paper, to play with it. Mother said, "No! That is money." Oh, money? I also said, 'Money' but I did not know, what this money was. "Money-money-money," I kept repeating. Thereafter, wherever I saw that green paper, I knew it was 'money' which I should not play with, but I did not know what money was.

Then, one day, when I was a little older, mother took me shopping with her to the store. I saw lots of chocolates and jellybeans. I stretched out

[1] $ US dollar

my hand, "Give me jellybeans." The man behind the counter raised his eyebrows and looked at mother. I wondered why he would not give me any candy when he had so many. Then mother opened her purse and pulled out a piece of green paper named money. When she gave that money to the storekeeper, he smiled and handed a packet of jellybeans to me. I did not understand what had happened, but I was happy with my jellybeans. The next time we went to the store, she gave money and the man gave me chocolates. One day when we were shopping, I wanted a balloon. Out came the money and the balloon was mine. Oh, ho! If you give money you can get jellybeans, chocolates, and even balloons. This was a great discovery for a small child. It had learnt that money buys things, all manner of things. Not many people understand the monetary system but everybody knows that money buys.

Later, as I grew up, I came to learn how many things money buys—houses, cars, even *guru*s and Gods. Nothing buys like money. When I come to know how well money buys, how many things money buys, I come to have a well-understood, well-assimilated personal value for money.

HALF VALUE IS MORE AN IRRITANT THAN BEHAVIOUR NORMS

When a universal value is split into two—a personal value for what I expect from others and an obligatory value for what I expect from myself—there is always a potential for conflict. While a personal value is spontaneously observed for its own sake, an obligatory value is subject to compromise when it obstructs a highly desired individual end. When a general ethical half-value loses the battle to an expedient-assimilated value, the half-value does not fold up and go away. It stays there as an irritant. What I call my ethical values, in fact, are often so many irritants in my heart. This is true even for the habitual offender who seems to be totally insensitive to the ethical behaviour standards. No matter what choices are made or how many times they are made, the voice of the half-value, reflecting as it does an inherent universal content, is never entirely silenced.

For example, most of us have a well-assimilated personal value for money; whereas, when it comes to speaking the truth, our value, often, is general and half assimilated. When this is the case, what happens if there is a conflict between the money-value and the truth-value? What if a situation arises whereby telling a lie I can make an extra 500 rupees? Suppose, someone has offered to pay me the same amount of money for an item that I had originally paid for it. I had paid 1000 rupees but I easily can say that I paid 1500 rupees. For this small lie I will gain an extra 500 rupees. I know what those extra 500 rupees can do for me, what comforts I can buy with it. On the other hand, it is not very clear to me of what benefit speaking truth in this situation will be to me. Should I tell the truth or should I lie? Which value will win? Very likely the assimilated value for money will be the victor. All the same, something goes on murmuring inside, "Speak the truth; speak the truth."

I may lie but I will not be comfortable, because I will not be able to avoid what happens when I tell a lie. What happens is that at first, there is conflict; then there is guilt. I can ignore the guilt but I cannot avoid guilt because I cannot escape my half-value for truth. Guilt is a great irritant, greater than chillies. Once I have guilt I cannot have a fully comfortable self. Fulfilling an immediate end at the expense of a general value may bring some passing comfort but, in the long run, it adds to my discomfort by increasing my accumulation of guilt, large and small.

THE KNOWER-DOER SPLIT

Does anything else happen when I ignore general ethical standards? Yes, I create a 'knower-doer' split in myself. For instance, when I lie I become a speaker. Speaking is an action, so as a speaker I am a doer. At the same time, I know what I am saying. I am aware that what I am saying is something contradictory to truth. Therefore, I, the knower, am in one position and I, the doer, am in another position. By my lie I create a split, a division, between the knower-I and the doer-I. Everyone has a few lies like these: What is your age? What is your income? What are your qualifications? When I build up a series of lies such as these, I create a split in myself, the knower being one and the doer being the other. I am not integrated.

I have divided myself into an ideal knower who values one course of action and the actual doer who does something else. I have created a Dr. Jekyll and Mr. Hyde conflict within myself. Living with Jekyll and Hyde, one cannot get anything out of life. It is impossible. Even in small things, the knower-doer split does harm. The knower decides to get up 30 minutes early and do early morning exercises. The doer turns off the alarm and sleeps 45 minutes longer. The knower goes on a diet. The doer has a second helping. I begin condemning myself. I tell myself that, I am useless, that I cannot do what I want to do, that I am not the person I want to be.

When I am 'split' I cannot fully enjoy anything. I cannot enjoy food unless the mind is on the food. The relationship between thinker and doer, perhaps, is more recognised in the Indian cultural traditions than it is in the West. In India the mother instructs the child, "Eat and don't talk. When you are eating, eat. Talk later." In the West talking is mixed with eating, only the first spoonful of food is appreciated. The rest of eating becomes mechanical. We eat and talk and then when we find that we cannot eat any more, we infer that the meal was good and that we have eaten a sufficient amount. The thinker was not present while eating, being too busy thinking what was to be said next. This kind of eating is mechanical and often uncontrolled, whereas, eating when the thinker is there alongside, can become an enjoyable ritual.

The quality of my life always suffers whenever I become a split. To appreciate the beauty of life, really to be available to enjoy its comforts, I need to be 'together'. 'Together' is a good western expression, which shows an intuitive appreciation of the problem of split. When my universal values are only half-values, they will always have the potential of destroying my togetherness, producing a split in me when they yield to some immediate situational value.

WHAT IS THE SOURCE OF A SITUATIONAL VALUE'S VALUE?

How does an individual situational value have the power to surmount the obligatory half of a universal value, which produces guilt and splits in me? We have seen that the source of ethical values is the natural desire that people treat me in a certain way, which then is extended and obliges me to treat others in the same way. What is the source of a situational value? Let us take our value for money. What gives money such a value that I may be willing to tell a lie to obtain it? In the example given above what is gained that makes the lie worthwhile to me? Is money a valuable thing worth a lie?

I cannot eat money or admire its beauty or talk to it or use it as shelter from the rain. Therefore, money itself is not the attraction, but with money I can buy things to eat, to wear, to look at and so on. Money itself is not valuable but the value of money seems to be in its buying power. However, if I were stranded on a desert island, the buying power of money would do me no good. Thus, it seems it must be the things themselves which money buys that make money valuable, not merely the isolated buying power. Why are the things valuable? The things are valuable for me, for my pleasure, security and comfort.I value things for my comfort.

What defines my comfort? Is it the 'me with comforts' that is valuable or the 'me' who feels comfortable? Is there a difference between the two? There is a difference. Sometimes, my stomach may be comfortably full, I am out of the rain, nothing is pinching, the heater is working and my chair is soft, yet I may not be comfortable with myself. What I really value is not mere comforts outside but to be comfortable with myself. It is always my hope that the extra comforts that money can buy for me, will make me more comfortable with myself. I buy comforts only for my sake, not for the sake of the comforts. I do not buy another chair because the chairs in the room are lonely. I buy a chair because, in one way or another, I think that to have a chair is going to make me feel more comfortable, either my body or pride of possession or both. All comforts are for my sake alone. I choose comforts for me so that I will feel good.

When I ignore my obligatory value for truthfulness, and tell a lie instead to gain some money, it is because I have concluded that the money will add to my comfort. I do not see, in the given instance, truthfulness doing anything for my comfort. The same is true for my other situational choices. Anything I choose, anything I value is because I think there is some connection between that thing and my feeling good. The source of the value of a situational value is that I expect to feel good by exercising a choice based on that value.

When is a value not subject to choice?

When I clearly see that a particular choice will make me suffer, I do not make that choice. When seeking comfort if I see between two choices, one of them is going to bring discomfort then I drop that choice. My action becomes choiceless like the answer to the question, "Do you want happiness or unhappiness?" Similarly, if I am thoroughly convinced that acting contrary to a general value will result in my suffering, my compliance with that value becomes choiceless. If speaking truth is a value for me and I am completely convinced that non-truth brings suffering, there is no choice but to speak truth. Speaking truth becomes natural, spontaneous and my personal assimilated value.

Any value, when it becomes my personal value, becomes choiceless for me. I do not have to think about it. The conduct mandated by a personal value is spontaneous, without reflection. Matters of hygiene are good everyday examples of personal assimilated values. Even if I am very hungry, I will not consider picking food from a garbage heap; nor, do I have a daily debate with myself over whether to brush my teeth or take a bath. I have no conflict in conforming to these values.

Seeing the Value of a Value

A value, any value, universal or situational, is a value for me only when I see the value of the value as valuable to me. I, the comfortable I, is the source of my values. I fail to follow a universal value only when I do not clearly see its value to me. I make expedient situational choices only when I think such choices will make me feel good.

Coming back to the 500 rupees that I gained by a small lie, what is the real worth of that lie to me? That small lie, joining its fellows in my mind, would cost me my mental comfort. The extra comforts that I could buy with the 500 rupees will not be able to deliver their comforts because of guilt and split. Guilt comes because I have a half-value for truth which, when I ignore it, creates a problem for me. Split comes because I know I am obliged to tell the truth and I am doing something else. Once I have guilt, once I am split, I cannot be comfortable with myself.

For comforts to be enjoyed I must be there to enjoy them. When I am split with guilt, I am rarely anywhere but with my anxieties, regrets and guilt. Not recognising the problem for what it is, I seek more comforts to ease my uncomfortable mind; or, I try to find some method for turning off this conflicting mind and its brood of guilt. Hence, when I tell a lie, I add to my discomfort when what

I was trying to gain by the lie was to add to my comfort. This is true for any choice I make which conflicts with a universal ethical standard. Since I made a conflicting choice, I cannot enjoy the sought-for comfort, because of the guilt and split arising from the conflict. When I clearly see this fact, I will see the value of applying universal ethical standards to myself. My half-value for universal values will become full value.

Life expression comes from value structure

The expression of my life is just the expression of my well-assimilated value structure. What I do is but an expression of what is valuable to me. I follow other people's values from time to time when it is convenient; but if these values have not been assimilated by me, they become simply obligatory values and do not reflect my value structure. They are more a source of conflict than a norm for behaviour and are always susceptible to compromise. Only assimilated values are my personal values. Assimilated values reflect what is valuable to me. An assimilated personal value requires no choice on my part. When I want certain unassimilated values to become part of my value structure, I must exercise deliberation in following them until I am convinced of their value to me. Their observance will become spontaneous for me, for which I must see its value in my personal life.

Paying lip service to obligatory values is no more useful than the chorus of parrots in a tree, who were singing out, "Be careful of the hunter's net!" A wise old parrot had seen the hunter coming and had called out the warning. The silly flock, however, did not look at the ground to spot the hunter, to understand the fact of the situation, to establish a personal content for the words they had heard from the old bird. Instead, they continued to sit happily on the branches of the tree repeating the words, empty of any real meaning for them: "Be careful of the hunter's net!" Even after the net had descended upon them, they wriggled and squirmed, caught in its web, screeching: "Be careful of the hunter's net!"

When I claim, as my standards, values in which I fail to see any personal gain, I am in as risky a position insofar as expressing those values, as were the parrots in the tree, mindlessly repeating the words. Enjoined or obligatory values will become assimilated personal values only when I see their value for me clearly and assimilate these values in terms of knowledge.

For the person with assimilated ethical values, life becomes very simple. No conflicts cloud his or her mind. For such a person, the teaching of Vedanta is like the meeting of gas and fire; knowledge ignites in a flash.

Twenty Values of an Enlightened Mind

In response to Arjuna's question, 'What is *jñāna*?' the values necessary to prepare the mind for knowledge are set out in the Bhagavad Gītā. Chapter xiii of the *Gītā* begins with Arjuna asking Lord Kṛṣṇa to teach him. In some *Gītā* manuscripts this opening verse is not found.

Arjuna *uvāca*

> *prakṛtiṁ puruṣaṁ caiva kṣetraṁ kṣetrajñam eva ca*
> *etad veditumicchāmi jñānaṁ jñeyaṁ ca keśava*

Arjuna said: Oh Lord! I would like to learn about: *prakṛti,* insentient matter and *puruṣa,* sentient person; *kṣetra,* the field, which indicates the body, and *kṣetrajña,* the knower who is conscious of the field, the body; *jñāna,* knowledge and *jñeya,* that which is to be known.

In answer to a part of the request, Lord Kṛṣṇa enumerates twenty qualities of the mind, which he terms '*jñāna*' or knowledge:

> *amānitvam adambhitvam ahiṁsā kṣāntirārjavam*
> *ācāryopāsanaṁśaucaṁsthairyamātmavinigrahaḥ* (13.7)

1. *Amānitvam* – absence of conceit
2. *Adambhitvam* – absence of pretence
3. *Ahiṁsā* – not hurting
4. *Kṣāntiḥ* – glad acceptance
5. *Ārjavam* – rectitude
6. *Ācāryopāsanam* – service to the teacher
7. *Śaucam* – inner and outer purity
8. *Sthairyam* – steadfastness
9. *Ātmavinigrahaḥ* – mastery over the mind

indriyārtheṣu vairāgyam anahaṅkāra eva ca
janmamṛtyujarāvyādhiduḥkhadoṣānudarśanam (13.8)

10. *Indriyārtheṣu vairāgyam* – dispassion towards sense objects
11. *Anahaṅkāraḥ* – absence of self-importance
12. *Janma-mṛtyu-jarā-vyādhi-duḥkha-doṣānu-darśanam* – Reflection on the limitations of birth, death, old age, sickness and pain

asaktiranabhiṣvaṅgaḥ putradāragṛhādiṣu
ṇityaṁ ca samacittatvam iṣṭāniṣṭopapattiṣu (13.9)

13. *Asaktiḥ* – absence of a sense of ownership
14. *Anabhiṣvaṅgaḥ putra-dāra-gṛhādiṣu* – absence of obsession to son, wife, house and so on

15. *Nityaṁ samacittatvam iṣṭa-aniṣṭa-upapattiṣu* – constant equanimity towards desirable and undesirable results

mayi cānanyayogena bhaktiravyabhicāriṇī
viviktadeśasevitvam aratirjanasaṁsadi (13.10)

16. *Mayi ananya-yogena bhaktiḥ avyabhicāriṇī* – unswerving devotion to Me characterised by non-separateness from Me

17. *Viviktadeśasevitvam* – preference for a secluded place

18. *Aratiḥ janasaṁsadi* – absence of craving for social interaction

adhyātmajñānanityatvaṁ tattvajñānārthadarśanam
etajjñānam iti proktam ajñānaṁ yadato 'nyathā (13.11)

19. *Adhyātma-jñāna-nityatvam* – Understanding the ultimate validity of Self-knowledge.

20. *Tattva-jñānārtha-darśanam* – Commitment to Self- knowledge

These are declared to be knowledge and what is opposed to it is ignorance.

As we have seen, 'knowledge' as used here does not mean knowledge of the self but stands for those qualities that prepare the mind for the knowledge of the self. Knowledge of the self in this verse is indicated by *jñeya,* that which is to be known. *Jñāna* indicates those qualities of the mind that must be present for the *vastu,* the truth, to be known. The truth is that which is the ultimate reality to be known, that which cannot be resolved into anything else.

We have seen in the previous discussion that for values to be personally valuable, they must be discovered through knowledge and not forced upon a person. Therefore, the term '*jñāna*' is quite appropriate. The list of values constituting *jñāna* is long but the qualities are interrelated. They define a harmonious frame of mind in which knowledge can occur. Each of the terms used by Lord Kṛṣṇa highlights a certain attitude, the value for which must be discovered personally, in order that the attitude becomes a natural aspect of the seeker's mind.

Amānitvam

Amānitvam is the first value listed. This word comes from the Sanskrit word *mānaḥ*, which means self-respect, self-esteem, extending to conceit or haughtiness. Thus, *mānaḥ* means an exaggerated opinion about oneself. *Mānaḥ* does not imply that one is without qualifications but rather that whatever qualifications one has, loom large in one's mind as worthy of respect and regard from others. The one who has *mānaḥ* is a *mānī*. The addition of *tvam* to *mānī* creates the abstract noun *mānitvam*, which stands for the essence of the quality, that is, for exaggerated self-respectfulness or self-conceit. The prefix '*a*' negates the meaning of the word; so, *amānitvam* indicates the absence of self-conceit.

A simple factual self-respectfulness is not a harmful quality of the mind; in fact, it is a good quality. A problem arises only when self-respectfulness is exaggerated into conceit. When self-respect becomes self-conceit, exaggerated, it does not just undesirably affect my attitude towards myself, but it manifests in my demand upon others to show me the respect that I feel is my due. When I demand respect from others, I invite many disturbances into my mind. I will not get or will rarely get the respect I demand and that too, on my terms. The person upon whom I make such a demand may not respond, or the person has his or her *mānitva*, and hence will respond with hostility or will demand a greater respect from me. The result can be mutual hurt, friction, and troubled minds.

WHAT IS THE BASIS FOR MĀNITVA?

What makes me demand respect from others? I have good qualifications and have a firm respect for them. However, the cause for demanding respect from others does not lie in my qualifications. The cause is found in the deep, underlying doubt in my mind about my qualifications. When I am very certain that I have, in full measure, the qualifications that I claim, I don't have the need to demand respect from others for those qualifications. No matter how strange or polysyllabic my name is, I do not demand respect from others for my ability to spell my name. In fact, commendation for this skill would be insulting. I take this ability for granted and do not concern myself with it.

Mānītva arises because I am doubtful about my qualifications. I do not seem to accept myself as one who is qualified. The demand upon others for recognition shows that I need some support so that I can feel that I am somebody. This demand comes from an inner sense of emptiness, a lack of readiness to accept myself as I am because I secretly fear that what I am is not good enough. Although I assert my qualifications, I am really all too conscious of my limitations. I am afraid to acknowledge limitations and of others acknowledging them. I want a response from others not to my limitations but only to my qualifications. Further, I want a response to my qualifications in the glorified light in which I view them.

Demand for respect leads to hurt

People respect others for various reasons. Sometimes respect is given solely because the person is in a position of power. In such cases if the position comes to an end, so does the respect. Other times respect is given because there is some genuine appreciation of qualities in the other person. However, the respect voluntarily given is subject to the whim of the giver. What he finds convenient to give one day may be too much the next. Also, the giver may cease his respectfulness if it is not returned to him in kind. If he too has an ego that requires extravagant support, he may find it deflating to extend support to another without reciprocity. A relationship in which there is a mutual demand for respect is likely to become a tug-of-war all the time. The result is mutual hurt.

Hurt caused by an inflated ego

Hurt is possible only when there is an inflated ego, pride. If you analyse any form of hurt, you will find it is only due to pride. Inflated ego is a disproportionate, excessive significance attached to what I know, what I feel, what I possess, what I do, how I look and so on. With this overemphasis on a 'knower-doer-I' comes the expectation of a certain response from others recognising my importance, seeing me, as I want to be seen. When that response does not come, I get hurt. A hurt, deflated ego tends to spend a lot of time planning how to retaliate, how to teach a lesson to those who hurt. Since a proud ego picks up lot of hurts, the list of those to be taught a lesson is likely to be long. Such a person cannot sit quietly in meditation. In the firmament of the mind of a person with a hurt ego the luminaries are all the people who caused the hurt. It is upon them that one dwells in meditation!

HURT IS ALWAYS A MONKEY'S WOUND

There is a proverb that says a wounded heart is like a monkey's wound. It does not heal but only gets reopened. A hurt mind may seem to be healed and then a sudden shadow crosses the face as the hurt is recalled to memory and the hurt reopens. Like clouds before the sun, gloom closes in. There is no time for Vedanta in the mind of a person who is always nursing hurts; one who demands respect accumulates many hurts to nurse.

QUALIFICATIONS SHOULD SPEAK FOR THEMSELVES

It is good to have abilities and to use them; but abilities should be allowed to speak for themselves. My attitude towards my accomplishments should be like a flowering bush towards its blossoms. In the city or in the wilderness, seen or unseen, praised or censured, the bush puts forth its blooms, colourful and fragrant. No publicity circulars are sent out to announce the blooming. The bush simply blooms because it is meant to bloom; it must. This is how I should be about my gifts and skills. These abilities seem to have come with me; why, I do not know. I should simply use them as well as I can because that is what I am supposed to do. People, who have a value for these particular abilities may respect me for them if circumstances are right for them to do so. People, who have no value for these particular abilities will, no doubt, ignore them. Both these attitudes should not make any difference to me. I should let my actions command respect from those who are able and willing to extend it but I cannot afford to demand respect.

Mānitva ceases when its foolishness is seen

How can I obtain the attitude of *amānitva,* the absence of *mānitva,* a demand for inordinate respect from others? *Amānitva* is obtained by losing *mānitva*. I do not have *amānitva* because *mānitva* has become a value for me, although, no doubt, I would not own up to this. *Mānitva* is a value for me because I think that by receiving large amounts of respect from others I will feel good about myself. *Mānitva* will cease to be a value for me when I clearly see, for myself, that the basis is false, and moreover, that it does not work.

We have already seen some of the reasons for, why a demand for respect does not work. Not everyone will have a value for my particular qualifications. Even if one has a value for my qualifications, one need not show respect to me because of one's own ego needs. One will show respect according to his or her convenience, mood and whim. It is often not easy to decode another person's attitude from his or her manner. If I am obsessed with the amount of respect I receive from another, I can waste a lot of time trying to analyse the other person's words and gestures and still not know his or her real attitude towards me. A curt manner may conceal a real value for the other person's qualifications. A rejecting manner may mask a real attitude of respect, which is clouded by jealousy or competitiveness. Further, I waste a lot of my time because of my concern with the respectful attitudes of others. Besides, there are so many factors that affect people's attitudes, factors that have no bearing on the true value of my qualifications. In any event, I may truly be unable to read the attitude of others from their manner or words.

If I will take the time to analyse the factors involved, I will see clearly that demanding respect from others is not likely to bring me much comfort or satisfaction, in spite of the reality of my qualifications. In addition to this insight, a further understanding of the absurdity of demanding respect from others will come if I examine the basis of the qualifications for which I want respect.

Mānitva is never justified by accomplishments

Mānitva is born because I do not understand the nature of accomplishments. I am proud of my achievements only because I consider myself the author of the acts, the producer of the skills or gifts. It does not take much analysis to smash this illusion. If I start by analysing my physical body, I did not author the body that houses me. It came to me with certain inherent potential or predisposition. Even if I subscribe to a belief in reincarnation and consider this body a vehicle shaped by my *karma*s, I can claim neither authorship nor knowledge of the particular laws that ordained this body. I do not know whether this particular body reflects more my overt actions in past lives or my parents' subtle actions, their prayers for a healthy, intelligent child at the inception of this life. Moreover, I cannot trace this body back to some first or originating body in a karma-sustained cause and effect chain of bodies. My apparent separate individuality, housed in this particular body, is without beginning, like the creation itself of which it is a part. I am not the author of creation, nor am I the author of my body. Therefore, whatever possibilities I have, appear to have been provided to me. I can exploit these abilities but I did not create them.

Even in the exploitation of my skills, sheer ability often is not the determinant of success or failure. When I look at any achievement I find that it is there because of certain opportunities I had, as well as because of my personal effort. I cannot claim to have created or commanded the opportunities; they were given to me. I happened to find myself in the right circumstances, and so I could grow and learn what I needed to learn. I met with the right person; happened to read the right book; I enjoyed the right company; someone came forward with the right guidance at the right time. There are so many factors behind an achievement. I cannot really say I created any of them. When I look at the facts, I must see that any achievement that I claim as mine is not due to my will or skill alone but it is due to certain things and opportunities that were provided to me. When I see the nature of accomplishment for what it is, there is no place for *mānitva*. In fact, I should be grateful for whatever abilities I seem to have. My demand for respect from others will go away when I see its foolishness.

How can I help myself see the foolishness of mānitva?

If I assume the position of a dispassionate analyst, ready to spot and analyse *mānitva* every time it pops up, it will soon disappear from my mind. The moment it appears, I recognise it for what it is and examine it carefully until I understand its foolishness in the particular circumstance. With practice, *mānitva* will lose its value for me. When I see its foolishness, that it no longer serves any purpose, it should drop off.

To be effective, I must analyse *mānitva* without self-condemnation or regret. I try to be objective, matter-of-fact, to see things as they are. When someone fails to respond to me in the way I would want them to, I merely observe my reactions without further reaction. From the position of an observer I see the senselessness of my expectations in all their absurdity. In addition, I see that what I really want is not an expression of respect from others for its own sake but because I hope that such an expression will make me feel more comfortable about myself. I see that my real problem is my basic feeling of inadequacy and self-doubt which is made worse, not better, by harbouring *mānitva*.

Mānitva is mithyā's mithyā

There are many things that are apparent, *mithyā*. In fact, all perceivable things are *mithyā*. *Mithyā* is that which enjoys a dependent rather than an absolute reality. This dependent reality, called *mithyā*, which characterises creation, usually is translated into English by the word 'apparent' by which it is meant to indicate that the reality is not absolute but is subject to negation.

All things objectified in the creation are *mithyā*; they begin and end and they can be resolved in ever finer, progressive resolutions into constituents. However, although subject to negation, apparent things still enjoy a certain level of reality. *Mānitva*, the ego, on the other hand, which manifests as pride, does not enjoy even an apparent reality.

Mānitva is *mithyā*'s *mithyā*. When I see this pride itself is *mithyā, mānitva* loses its meaning. When *mānitva* goes away, what remains is *amānitva*. *Amānitva* is not developed; *mānitva* is eliminated. *Amānitva* is very natural. When I enjoy *amānitva* I become a simple person. A simple person is one who does not have any complexities.

Mānitva goes when its foolishness is seen. It is not a practical advice to be told to give up pride or ego. Irrational as it may be, a proud ego is very common; particularly in a society where individualism has come to be so highly prized, pride is a problem.

Emphasis on individualism makes a person prouder and more subject to the hurts that go with pride. However, in the light of knowledge, pride, *mānitva,* appears silly and I will be able to keep the ego to the level necessary to conduct my affairs. I then enjoy *amānitva,* a quality of mind conducive to the discovery of the self.

Adambhitvam

Adambhitva is the mental state in which *dambha* is absent. *Dambha* is an attitude that results in an expression quite similar to that of *mānitva;* it manifests as self-glorification. However, between the two, the foundation for the expression differs. *Mānitva*'s conceit is an expression based on real achievements and abilities; whereas, the claim to fame caused by *dambha* stems from pretended or fabricated accomplishments and abilities. *Dambha* means pretence or feigning. The *dambhī* is one who claims achievements that are not his or pretends to possess abilities which he or she does not have.

It is called *dambha* when I trumpet my glory that is not there. It is *dambha* when by design I give the impression that I am somebody, which I know I am not. It is an expression of *dambha* by dress, *veṣa,* when I dress as if I were a wealthy person when, in fact, my bank account is overdrawn and I am dodging bill collectors. It is an expression of *dambha* by words, *bhāṣā,* when I claim recognition as a scholar, alluding to papers or books that have been published or that are about to be published, when in fact all I have ever written are letters to relatives asking for loans.

Causes of dambhitva

When I give expression to *dambhitva* it is because I think that through my pretences I will impress others who will then respond to me in a way that will make me feel good. *Dambhitva* arises because I do not feel good about myself. I do not accept myself as I am. I want to be different. I find myself unacceptable. So, in order that others too will not find me unacceptable, I present myself as I think I would like to be or in a way that I think will impress others.

Dambhitva requires a long memory

We have seen the reasons why *mānitva,* a self-conceited demand for respect from others, is a foolish attitude. These reasons apply to *dambhitva* also. There is no way to compel others to respond favourably to my accomplishments, whether the accomplishments are real or fancied. In the case of *dambhitva,* there is no problem in seeing that I cannot claim authorship of the accomplishments, which I publicise, inasmuch as they are a pretence and not a fact. In addition, *dambhitva* is particularly absurd because it is able to bring even less comfort than *mānitva* to the mind which harbours it; instead it brings a load of tension. It brings tension because the *dambhī* must always be on guard against being 'found out'. Here is an incident to illustrate this point. A man asked his friend, "Where have you been? I haven't seen you around for a long time." The *dambhī* replied, "I have been in the capital. The PM wanted some regional input on the tax-reform proposal." When the *dambhī*'s wife appeared, he hastily ended the conversation before she could reveal that he had gone out of town only to help his brother-in-law to move house. *Dambhitva* brings with it the need to be ever alert and to have a long memory. Truth does not require special efforts to remember.

Dambhitva is a big problem for the mind

The mind being what it is, there is always a tendency, in small measure, for *dambhitva*. I always tend to present myself somewhat better than I am. This attitude is not conducive to the frame of mind that is receptive to the teaching of Vedanta. Any *dambhitva* is a commitment to falsehood. A mind committed to falsehood cannot be a happy, quiet mind available for learning. In particular, a mind which expresses *dambhitva,* is non-receptive to the messages of wisdom that one's life experiences unfold. When I suffer from *dambhitva,* I do not accept myself, instead, I commit myself to an image that I know is false; whereas, the reality of intelligent living calls for owning up myself as I am. Basically, if I deeply reject myself as the attitude of *dambhitva* indicates, I will have a very difficult time accepting and assimilating the knowledge of the truth of myself. The truth of the self that Vedanta reveals to me is that I lack nothing. Vedanta shows me that the multiplicity of creation is but *mithyā,* apparent, and that the non-dual reality of myself is limitlessness, fullness. However, to be ready for this teaching, which will reveal to me my limitlessness, I must enjoy a mind that accepts me as I am, right now, with all my apparent limitations.

SELF-ACCEPTANCE PREPARES THE MIND FOR VEDANTA STUDY

To be ready for the study of Vedanta, I should be able to accept myself just as I think I am and be willing to present myself to myself as I am. I should be free of self-condemnation. I should like myself as I am; at the same time I have a strong desire to find absolute freedom, free from the limitations that seem to bind me. When I suffer from *dambhitva,* it is scarcely possible for me to have a true desire to be free. My commitment to falsity and the deep rejection of my relative self, falsifies even a desire for freedom.

When *dambhitva* goes, the mind will enjoy the state of *adambhitva,* the absence of hypocrisy and pretence. With such a mind I become a real person. A real person is a simple person, while the complex person is false. A simple person may not be without problems. He may get angry. He may make mistakes. However, in his simplicity and straight-forwardness, he is able to get rid of his anger, learn from his reactions. For the false person committed to pretence, there is no learning, only hiding and tension.

When I clearly see the futility and absurdity of both the attitudes of *mānitva* and *dambhitva,* these negative values will drop off, leaving me with a mind reflecting *amānitva* and *adambhitva,* the absence of pride and the absence of pretence. No scripture or master can help a person with a mind ruled by pride and pretence. A mind that is simple and factual is the one that is ready to discover the truth of the self.

Ahiṁsā

Ahiṁsā comes from the Sanskrit verb '*hiṁs*' which means 'to hurt, injure or cause harm.' *Ahiṁsā,* not hurting or non-harmfulness, reflects my inherent desire to live free of hurt or pain or threat of any sort. Even thoughts can cause pain. If I know that someone harbours hurtful thoughts about me, although they are not expressed in word or deed, it pains me. *Ahiṁsā* means not causing harm by any means, neither by thoughts, *manasā,* nor by words, *vācā,* nor by deeds, *kāyena.*

Why should I not hurt other beings? It is because I do not want to be hurt. Common sense ethics dictate that I cannot do to another what I do not want done to me. So *ahiṁsā,* not hurting, becomes a value for me. *Ahiṁsā* is simple common sense *dharma,* confirmed by the Vedas and all the scriptures but subject to interpretation. If an injurious act benefits another, such as the cut of the surgeon's knife, it is not *hiṁsā.* In a relative world where one life form feeds on another, absolute *ahiṁsā* is not possible. Therefore, this is a value, which particularly requires understanding and interpretation.

VEGETARIANISM IS AN EXPRESSION OF AHIṀSĀ

Vegetarianism is an example of the application of the value for *ahiṁsā*. Many arguments in favour of a vegetarian diet can be made, but the basic argument supporting non-flesh eating is simply *ahiṁsā*. In India, where there are more vegetarians than anywhere else in the world, vegetarianism is squarely based on the Vedic mandate, "*hiṁsāṁ na kuryāt,* do not cause injury."

Why is more *hiṁsā* involved in eating an egg than an eggplant, or a steak than a pumpkin? Every life form requires food of some kind. One life form feeds upon another. What is tragedy to a bird is dinner to a cat. This being the case, why should not a human being also eat meat? Since a human being is not in the same choiceless category as the canary-eating cat, he or she cannot use the cat's example to justify his food habits. For the cat and other non-human life forms, choosing what to have for dinner is not a problem. They select their proper food by instinct. They come pre-programmed with their particular dietary knowledge; they need only to locate it. This is not so with a human being. He or she is a self-conscious being, endowed with a free will. This means he or she can choose from many means to fulfil his or her ends, including the basic need, food. Since he or she is not pre-programmed, a human being must choose the kind of food he or she eats.

Several arguments other than *ahiṁsā* are offered to support the position that vegetarianism is a better diet than meat eating. There is evidence that human dental and digestive systems are more suitable for a fruit-grain-vegetable diet than for meat. There is statistical evidence that vegetarians, such as the Seventh Day Adventists, have fewer degenerative diseases and live long enjoying a more vigorous old age, than do their meat-eating neighbours. However persuasive these arguments may be, the fundamental argument in favour of vegetarianism is the value of *ahiṁsā*.

ALL CREATURES SEEK TO LIVE A HARM-FREE LIFE

It is obvious that all living beings have a value for life. Anything that is alive tries to stay alive, including plants and very simple life forms. However, it is also obvious that all beings do not seem to have the same relative level of awareness of life, the same conscious ability to perceive threats to life or to struggle to preserve life.

Creatures in the animal kingdom are closer than plants to the human being in their awareness of threats to life and in their struggle to stay alive, if their behaviour indicates anything. Mobile creatures such as animals, birds, fish, run away from me when they know I am trying to catch them for the stew pot. When I do catch them, they struggle and scream. Therefore, I cannot but know that they do not want to be hurt, that they want to live. No mobile creature wants to be my dinner.

Since I have been given a free will to exercise a choice of food, which I eat to sustain my life, I must find some norm to guide me in choosing that food. The gift of free will carries with it a responsibility to follow an ethical norm in exercising that will. What is the common sense dharmic norm for choice of my food? The Veda tells me, *hiṁsāṁ na kuryāt,* do not cause injury. My common sense tells me that I should not make somebody my dinner since I do not want to be somebody's dinner. Who or what is a 'somebody'? Those living creatures who have the means to run away from me and my equipment, who scream in protest or struggle against me are more of a 'somebody' than plants. Plants are rooted in one place and quietly yield their fruits for my food, often without surrendering their lives. Anyway food chain starts with plant life. There is no other food except vegetarian. Even animals have to eat the vegetarian food, and then they get killed for meat. There is only a non-vegetarian meal but not non-vegetarian food; food being vegetarian.

PLANT FOOD IS THE RATIONAL AND ETHICAL CHOICE FOR HUMAN DIET

In view of the research indicating that a balanced vegetarian diet is complete and healthy, I cannot justify the use of meat in my diet on the basis of nutritional need. If I choose to eat meat, that choice is entirely my personal preference. To fulfil a preference is fine if there is no overriding ethical reason for not fulfilling it. In the case of eating meat, there is a strong common sense ethical reason for not fulfilling such a preference.

Since I do not want to be an animal's dinner, I should not make an animal my dinner. Plant food, rather than meat, is the choice because many plants seem designed to give up their produce as food for other life forms without surrendering their own lives. Another reason is that even when the use of plant food does destroy the plants, they appear to have less conscious appreciation of the threat or harm to themselves than animals do.

If I insist on including meat in my diet, to raise such a decision to ethical status, I would have to put myself on an equal footing with other carnivorous animals. To be on an equal footing, I should hunt and kill my prey barehanded without weapons, thus exposing myself to the possibility of being their dinner. If I am not willing to do so, the use of animals for food will be unethical. It will conflict with my half-value for not hurting. My failure to risk the possibility of suffering the same result reveals that I have such a half-value.

Ahiṁsā requires sensitivity and alertness

The value for *ahiṁsā* requires alertness and sensitivity in all areas of my life. It is a value that finds expression in my attitude towards plants as well as towards human beings and animals. Wanton destruction of plant life indicates a lack of sensitivity for the value of *ahiṁsā*. *Ahiṁsā* is a value for not destroying or damaging any part of creation, a creation of which I, too, am a part. I do not casually crush, strip, uproot or cut down plants. With regard to my fellow human beings, I watch for those words or acts or even thoughts that may be hurtful. I develop a finer appreciation for the feelings of others. I come to see beyond my own needs to the needs of those around me. I treat all things and beings with sensitivity and appreciate their common existence with me.

With such an attitude I become an alert, observant person with a sensitive, saintly mind that is ready to hear and appreciate the truth of Vedanta. *Ahiṁsā* is an important value among the values enumerated for gaining self-knowledge.

Kṣāntiḥ

The Sanskrit word *kṣānti,* often, is translated as forbearance or endurance. These two English words convey a slight negative connotation of resigned sufferance, whereas, *kṣānti* is a positive attitude, not painful resignation. A better translation is accommodation, acceptance. The attitude of *kṣānti* means that I cheerfully, calmly accept that behaviour and those situations, which I cannot change. I give up the expectation or demand that the other person or a situation should change in order to conform to what would be pleasing to me. I happily accept and accommodate situations and people.

All relationships require accommodation

This value must be built upon an understanding of the nature of people and relationships between them. I will never find in one person all the qualities that I like or dislike. Any given person is going to be a mixture of things, appealing and not appealing. Similarly, I am going to have the same impact on others. No one is going to find me totally likeable. When I recognise these facts, I see that every relationship requires some accommodation from me. Moreover, I may not be willing to change or be able to change to meet all the expectations that others have of me. Equally, the others are not going to change to meet all my expectations of them. Therefore, I will never find a relationship that does not require accommodation.

In particular, relationships wherein I strongly dislike certain aspects of a person require accommodation from me. If I can change the person or can put a distance between him or her and me without avoiding duty, it is not a problem. If I cannot, I simply must accommodate happily; I must take the person as he or she is. I can expect neither the world nor the people in it to change in order that I may be happy. It is just not possible to compel people to change to meet my image of what they should be like. Sometimes some may change a little for me or may try to change but I cannot count on this. More often than not, when I want change from others, they will just as strongly want change from me. It will be a face off between their image of me and my image of them.

Reduce expectations for kṣānti

When I examine my mental processes, to my surprise, I probably will find that I extend *kṣānti* more readily to a not-so-bright person than to my best friend. This is because I do not expect anything wise or intelligent from that person, whereas, I expect my friend to live up to certain standards that I consider appropriate. A not-so-bright person can never disappoint me but everyone else can, for one reason or another, at one time or another. This is not acceptable. As far as my expectations are concerned I should place everyone in the same category. No one should disappoint me but should only be able to surprise me. My attitude should be that I am prepared to accommodate and accept all surprises.

Hence, I accommodate people the same way as I accommodate inert objects; I take them as they are. I do not like to be over-baked by the summer sun but I do not ask the sun to stop shining. I appreciate the mixed blessing of a hot shining sun, and understand that, whether it is a mixed blessing or not, I cannot turn the sun off. I do not ask a honeybee to become sting-less nor do I hate honeybees if I get stung. I appreciate the role of the honeybee and enjoy honey.

However, I find it much harder to have the same attitude, which I have towards insects and inert objects, towards people. I am able to relate myself properly to an inert object or a wild creature because I do not expect any change from it. However, I expect people to be able to change, to become more pleasant to me. My mind is troubled with continuous demands for change so that others in my life will be more to my liking. Unfortunately, the reality is that people may not be able to change. Often, even if they do want to change, they cannot. When he or she does not change, even though willing to change, it only means that he or she has no strength of will. There is nothing we can do but accommodate such a person. When the other person does not change because he or she is not willing to try, one can attempt to convince the person of the desirability, of the need for change. If we cannot convince the person, there is nothing we can do except to accommodate him or her. We can say that the world is wide and large enough to accommodate all of us. Variety makes life more interesting.

RESPOND TO THE PERSON, NOT TO THE ACTION

In order to discover within myself a value for accommodation, I should look at the person behind the act. Usually, while responding to a person's behaviour, to the person's action, I find that it is difficult to be accommodative. However, when I try to understand the cause behind the action, I put myself in a position to respond to the person, not to the action, thereby my response to the person can be an accommodative response. I try to see what is behind the fit of anger or outburst of jealousy or domineering manner; I respond to the person and not to the actions. If I cannot see what is behind the actions, nonetheless I keep in mind the fact that many reasons, unknown to me, set the stage for the other person's action. With this frame of mind I find it natural to be accommodative. In a situation where my response is to the person rather than to the behaviour, I find myself staying calm. In fact, resolution of an argument between people is nearly always the result of the concerned parties' mutual appreciation as persons rather than any new attitude towards the precipitating behaviour.

Mechanical reactions block accommodation

To be free to respond to the person I must be free of mechanical reactions. I must choose my attitude and act deliberately. A reaction is a mechanical, non-deliberate sort of behaviour on my part. It is a conditioned response borrowed from previous experiences, one not given prior sanction by my will. It is a response, which I do not measure against the value structure that I am trying to assimilate, but I just allow it to happen. Sometimes my reaction may be an action or an attitude that I would do or hold after reflection, sanction. At other times, my reaction may be completely contrary to the attitudes and actions I would choose to hold or do.

Reactions can go against my wisdom, learning and prior experiences. These factors get relegated to the background and the reaction happens. All that I have previously learnt becomes worthless to me. I may have read the scriptures of the world, I may be a great student of ethical systems, I may be a professional degree-holding adviser, but when it comes to a reaction, it will be just as mechanical as anyone else's. Wisdom, learning, experience, will not count at all. Therefore, until I have thoroughly assimilated ethical values, which comprise a ground out of which right attitudes and actions spontaneously arise, I must avoid reactions with alertness. Instead, deliberately, reflectively I choose my attitudes and actions. When I avoid reactions, I am free to choose my actions and attitudes. I can choose to be accommodative in my thoughts, words and deeds.

KṢĀNTI AND AHIṀSĀ: QUALITIES OF A SAINT

Kṣānti, accommodation, is a saintly quality. Among all the qualities, *ahiṁsā* and *kṣānti* constitute the qualities, perhaps the minimum qualifications, of a saint. One need not have wisdom, one need not have scriptural learning to be a saint but one must have these two values. A saint is a person, who never consciously hurts another person by action, word or thought, who accepts people, good or bad, just as they are and who has an endless capacity to be accommodative, forgiving, merciful. These qualities, accommodation, forgiveness, mercifulness, are included in the quality called *kṣānti.* A saint always has *kṣānti,* an infinite capacity for compassion. He responds to the person, not to the action. He sees wrong action as a mistake born of inner conflict and is humane to the person who commits it. An attitude of *kṣānti*, accommodation, expands one's heart. The heart becomes so commodious that it accommodates all people and circumstances just as they are, without desire or demand that they be different. This is *kṣānti*.

Ārjavam

Ārjavam means 'straightness'. When used as a value, the 'straightness' or *ārjava* is similar to the English word rectitude from the Latin rectos, straight, which means conduct in accordance with one's ethical standards. So *ārjava* means an alignment of thought, word and deed. When there is *ṛjubhāva,* arrow-like straightness, between a physical action and the word, or between the word and the thought, that alignment is called *ārjava*.

What is non-alignment of thought, word and act? When I think one thing and say another or when I say one thing and do another or when I think one thing, say another and do even a third thing, all of these constitute a non-alignment on my part, of thoughts, words and deeds. The avoidance of this disconnection, this division between word and action, word and thought, and action and thought, is *ārjava*. *Ārjava* can be considered an extension of *satya-vacana,* truthful speech. *Ārjava* covers more ground; it includes not just *vacana,* speech, but also thoughts and actions. For *ārjava,* my actions must be true to my words and my words true to my thoughts.

Non-alignment results in a splintered person

What is the importance of alignment between thought, word and deed? By non-alignment I become disintegrated. I am no longer a whole person. When there is conflict between my values, my thoughts, my words and my acts, I suffer a destructive split in myself. I become splintered. I am not 'together'. If there is a gulf between me, the thinker, and me, the speaker or the doer, the result will be a restless mind troubled by guilt and conflicts. This kind of mind is not a quiet, receptive instrument ready for learning anything, for achieving any end. For such a mind, self-knowledge is a far cry. To be prepared to listen to the teaching of Vedanta, you need to be 'together', not split. Therefore, *ārjava,* the alignment of thought, word and deed is included as one of the values of *jñāna*.

Ācāryopāsanam

Ācāryopāsanam primarily means service to the teacher. This value is one that is deeply embedded in the Hindu culture. Its intensity and universality within the culture show the high regard for knowledge and for the teacher who imparts knowledge.

Ācāryopāsana also is used to indicate specific aspects of the student-teacher relationship. *Gurukulavāsa*, living with the teacher, for a length of time in a *gurukula* and learning from him, is called *ācāryopāsana*. 'Meditation upon the teacher' is another very literal meaning for *ācāryopāsana*. *Ācārya* means teacher and *upāsana* is meditation. Together these words form the Sanskrit compound *ācāryopāsana*. Meditation upon the teacher means meditation upon the teaching by keeping the *ācārya*, the teacher, who stands for the vision of the teaching, always in one's heart.

'Service and surrender', however, is the general meaning of *ācāryopāsana*. This is the sense in which Lord Kṛṣṇa uses the term when talking to Arjuna. In this sense, *ācāryopāsana* requires certain discrimination in its exercise. Care must be taken in choosing the teacher who will receive the service. Expression of *ācāryopāsana* can lead to exploitation of the value holder, if the teacher is not a responsible person.

Service to the teacher implies a whole frame of mind towards the teacher, a frame of mind characterised by surrender of personal ego, subordination of personal likes and dislikes, a willingness to give without demand for return, and a general attitude of respect and devotion. Thus, *ācāryopāsana* means a great personal surrender. This kind of surrender to another person should be made only when the person to whom surrender is made has no need for the surrender, no need for the service, no need of any kind, and no need to be the beneficiary of the attitude of *ācāryopāsana*. Only a person, who has a clear, steady knowledge of the truth of the self, is without needs. Such a person is one who can be a real teacher, a teacher who can unfold the knowledge of the self that is the ground of all knowledge, and to whom the student can surrender completely with no fear of exploitation. So, when Lord Kṛṣṇa tells Arjuna that *ācāryopāsana* is one of the values constituting *jñāna*, it is understood that the teacher, at whose feet the student surrenders, must be a teacher of such integrity and freedom from need for service that only the student, not the teacher, will be the beneficiary of surrender.

In *ācāryopāsana* willingness to serve is the significant aspect rather than the particular acts of service done. Willingness to serve means an inner readiness to serve whether or not we are called upon to serve. It means a happy acceptance of any way in which we are asked to serve, an attitude in which nothing asked of us is considered too small or large a service. In service, large is small and small is large. We are ready to do any action we can. In this teacher-student relationship there is no give and take as there is in other relationships. There is only giving on the part of the student. Through such an attitude of unquestioning, complete service the student becomes blessed. The teacher becomes an altar at which he or she can surrender.

Earlier, Lord Kṛṣṇa had told Arjuna:

> *Tadviddhi praṇipātena paripraśnena sevayā*
> *Upadekṣyanti te jñānaṁ jñāninastattvadarśinaḥ*
>
> (Gītā: 4.34)

> Know that by prostrating yourself, by inquiry and by service, the wise person, who knows the truth, will teach you that knowledge.

It is this description of discipleship that is embraced by the term *ācāryopāsana*. When the teacher is one true to his name and the nature of service is understood, *ācāryopāsana*, surrender to the teacher is a beautiful thing, blessing the student and making his mind receptive to the knowledge to be unfolded. In gaining any discipline of knowledge, respect for the teacher is an essential element.

Śaucam

Śaucam is cleanliness in a two-fold sense, *bāhya-śauca,* external cleanliness, and *āntara-śauca,* inner cleanliness. *Bāhya-śauca* is a well-understood universal value. It is easy to see the benefit that comes to me and to others from external cleanliness. Clean body, clean clothes, and clean dwelling places make life more pleasant. In addition, the daily discipline of maintaining cleanliness brings about a certain attentiveness and alertness of mind.

Āntara-śauca is less well-recognised. *Āntara-śauca* means cleanliness of the *antaḥkaraṇa,* mind. What is *aśauca,* uncleanliness of the mind? What makes a mind unclean? Jealousy, anger, hatred, fear, selfishness, self-condemnation, guilt, pride, possessiveness, all these emotions and the climate of despair and resentment which come in their wake, are the unclean qualities of the mind. Every day, while I go about my business, dust settles on my skin, dirt smudges my clothes, my desk becomes littered, and in my transactions with people and circumstances my mind gathers daily *aśauca*. Linked to my likes and dislikes, *rāga*s and *dveṣas*, smudges of envy settle, a spot of exasperation lands, streaks of possessiveness appear, and overall, the fine dust of self-criticism, guilt and self-condemnation spreads in my mind.

Each day I wash my body, launder my clothes and straighten my desk. It is a day-to-day affair until death. Until my body goes, I must do this. It is the same with the mind. Each day, until, in the knowledge of the self, my false identification with the mind goes, my mind must be cleaned. When there is no daily cleaning outside or inside, the accumulation makes the task much more difficult.

Pratipakṣa-bhāvanā, attitude to cleanse the mind

How can we clean the mind? What is the detergent for the mind? It is *pratipakṣa-bhāvanā*. *Prati*, a Sanskrit prefix, means 'opposite'; *pakṣa* stands for 'position' or 'point of view'. *Bhāvanā* indicates thinking or 'state of thought'. Thus, *pratipakṣa-bhāvanā* means a state of mind with the 'opposite point of view'. The practice of *pratipakṣa-bhāvanā* is to take, deliberately, the opposite point of view, by an act of will, to think the opposite of the unclean thoughts.

I undertake this opposite thinking and act accordingly, even though I feel that my attitude is justified. Someone may do an improper action that insults or injures me. Resentment settles in my mind. The action may have been inarguably improper, but the resentment nonetheless is mine; it is *aśauca* of my mind. If I allow it to remain, the resentment can build up into hatred, a painful disturbing mental state. When I see, therefore, the personal consequence of allowing *aśauca* to remain, when the object of resentment comes to my attention, I deliberately use my will to think of thoughts, opposite to the negative ones that first come to mind.

Banish resentment by seeing the saint

When I see a person I resent or dislike, not disliked by everyone, then I deliberately search for the reason why others like him. I think of the positive facts that I know of the person, that he is kind to his children, that he cares for his parents, that he gives to charity and so on. I call to mind the good things I know of him.

When I look into any person I will find love. I am capable of loving. Any person is capable of loving.

Even a person given to crime has within him the elements of love and sympathy. It may be that the criminal's capacity for love is so obscured that it only manifests itself in the sympathy he shows to himself, when he accidentally bangs his thumb with a hammer; but it is there to be discovered. Manifest or not, everyone has the qualities of compassion, mercy, love, not hurting and so on that makes one a saint. Therefore, to cleanse the mind of resentment and dislikes that solidify into hatred, I deliberately search for those things in another person that indicate his humaneness, his saintliness. They are there in everyone.

When you focus only on the glimpses of saintliness in another person, all the other traits you have observed in him are attributed merely to error, mistake, habit, wrong thinking, wrong environment, and wrong upbringing. You take it as your blessing that you are not in the same position that he is in. With the same parentage, the same environment, your own behaviour would be what you object to in him. You see behind the acts, the person possessed of all the saintly qualities, because innately these qualities are the human qualities. Saintly qualities are the qualities of the self, the qualities that really constitute human nature. The opposite qualities are incidental; they come and go.

When resentment, dislike, hatred towards someone arises, introduce thoughts that are their opposite. See the person behind the action from an opposite viewpoint, and you will discover in yourself some sympathy or understanding for that person. Your attitude will be one of *kṣānti*, accommodation towards him or her. In this manner, by deliberate, consistent practice, any resentment, any hatred that appears is erased, cleansed on a daily basis.

The Aśauca of Selfishness

Selfishness provides a good example of *aśauca* that yields to *pratipakṣa-bhāvanā*. In the case of selfishness, the *pratipakṣa-bhāvanā* thoughts often can be reinforced by action as well. When I see myself inconsiderate to the wants, needs, happiness of others, I can consciously programme myself to overdo in the opposite direction. Making myself alert to the needs and happiness of those around me, I can find ways to be considerate. Whenever I can do something that will compensate some selfish omission or commission on my part, I do so.

It not only settles and frees my mind from that account but also underlines, by deliberate action, the attitude of unselfishness that I wish to develop. When a decision to change an attitude is well expressed physically, that is, confirmed by action, it is hard for the negative opposite attitude to register in the mind again.

The aśauca of self-condemnation

Universal ethical values, consciously or unconsciously, remain as a matrix for self-judgement of any thought or action that transgress their standards. Whenever I fail to abide by a general value, some conflict usually registers in my mind. Conflict becomes guilt and guilt turns into an underground chorus of self-condemnation, *aśauca,* subtly pervading my mind.

Self-condemnation can be called subtle *aśauca* because, to many, it is not apparent that self-condemnation is *āntara-aśauca,* mental uncleanliness. In fact, those who are unaware of the truth of the self may regard self-condemnation as a useful goad to prod us to change our nature. This is not a correct or a useful understanding of ourselves or of the term self-condemnation. Condemnation of oneself cannot be justified anymore than condemnation of others. Both rest upon the faulty understanding of the self. Both produce turmoil in the mind.

Self-condemnation can be controlled by *pratipakṣa-bhāvanā,* by refusing to condemn myself while at the same time deliberately thinking non-self-condemning thoughts. Analysis of the nature of self-condemnation will help me exercise *pratipakṣa-bhāvanā*. On analysis I will always find that in this body-mind package, which I term 'I', the body that carries out the act cannot be condemned. The hands, the legs, the feet, the tongue and all the other parts of the body are inert, *jaḍa*. The body itself lacks self-consciousness or independent will. Similarly, the senses and the various functions of the body are not independent, conscious processes. Performing their jobs indiscriminately, either automatically or upon direction from the mind, they cannot be held culpable. Neither can the mind be labelled the culprit. The mind is not a simple, definable entity, but is an ever-changing aggregate of thoughts in motion, some beautiful, some not beautiful, and some useful, and some inconsequential. The mind, that thought the thought, which led to the act that I condemn, is now the same mind that thinks the thought that condemns the mind that thought before. Thus, the mind is an aggregate of available thoughts at a given point in time, in an on-going process characterised by constant change. The mind is only a process that performs as a useful instrument. It cannot be condemned. Then what can be condemned? Can *ātman,* the name for first-person-singular, I, be condemned? From the scripture, *śruti,* I know that *ātman* illumines the mind. *Ātman,* is *sat-cit-ānanda,* boundless, timeless, awareness, fullness, form-free, and action-free. Being neither the doer nor the enjoyer, neither a *kartā* nor a *bhoktā,* the *ātman* cannot be blamed.

Therefore, what can I condemn? I can condemn just a given thought, neither my body nor my mind nor my *ātman.* If there is anything that justifiably can be condemned, it is but a given thought born of ignorance and error, a thought that ordered an improper action.

Thus, if self-condemnation is analysed properly and we inquire into 'what-does-what', the result will not be condemnation of the self but condemnation, if any, of an act simply for what the act is and of the particular error-born thought behind the act. Clearing away the self-condemnation leaves the mind free to discover, as a personal value, the ethical norm that has been transgressed. The *aśauca* of regret is removed. If I have done the act, there is regret. If a particular thought has done it, freed from the sorrow of regret, I can address myself to understanding what gave rise to the thought.

In India, as small boys, each year on a special day we used to repeat the following Vedic mantra 1008 times:

> "*Kāmokārṣīnnamo namaḥ*
> *Kāmokārṣīt kāmaḥ karoti nāhaṅkaromi*
> *Kāmaḥ kartā nāhaṅkartā*
> *Kāmaḥ kārayitā nāhaṅkārayitā eṣa te*
> *kāma kāmāya svāhā*
>
> Desire did, salutations to you, Lord Desire
> Desire did, desire does; it is not I
> Desire is the doer, not I
> Desire causes the act, not I
> Salutations to you, Desire
>
> *Manyurakārṣīnnamo namaḥ*
> *Manyurakārṣīnmanyuḥ karoti nāhaṅkaromi*
> *Manyuḥ kartā nāhaṅkartā*

Manyuḥ kārayitā nāhaṅkārayitā eṣa te
manyo manyave svāhā

Anger did, salutations to you, Lord Anger
Anger did, anger does; it is not I
Anger is the doer, not I
Anger causes the act, not I
Salutations to you, Anger"

(Kṛṣṇayajurveda: Taittirīya Āraṇyaka)

Repetition of this *mantra,* even though only once a year, is a wonderful thing because there is no self-condemnation in it. At the same time, I know, I am aware that there were some actions that were not appropriate. I recognise that those actions had a certain basis in desire, or a basis in anger. Anger is thwarted desire born of ignorance or conditioning. When I recognise the basis of an action, be it desire or anger, it makes my mind alert. Alertness helps to break the conditioning; thereby making the mind receptive to the knowledge that dispels ignorance.

THE AŚAUCA OF JEALOUSY

In Sanskrit, jealousy is called *mātsarya. Mātsarya* is defined as, *parotkarṣaṁ dṛṣṭvā jāyamānaḥ santāpaḥ.*

Dṛṣṭvā, having seen, *utkarṣam,* the superiority of someone, *santāpaḥ,* a pain or sadness, *jāyamānaḥ,* that is born, is *mātsarya,* jealousy. It is the anguish, the pain that is born on seeing another's superiority or excellence.

Of all *aśauca,* jealousy is the most illegitimate of the attitudes because even by the standards of the relative world it is unreal. Most of the reactive attitudes, which are considered *aśauca,* are based on either the pursuit of or the threat, real or imagined, to some objective that is capable of being achieved, at least theoretically. It is not so with jealousy. Jealousy is a reaction of sorrow over a lack, which I conclude exists, when I compare myself with some other human being who is seen as superior. This supposed superiority, if it exists at all, when examined would always be found as partial, incomplete. Upon close examination, the one who is jealous would never be able to consider the aggregation of parts and functions that constitute the entity, the object of jealousy, totally superior. If I am jealous I will never be jealous of all the aspects of another person; nor will anyone who is jealous of me find me totally superior. Since the endowments, skill, grace, possessions that inspire my jealousy cannot be separated from the entire entity; and since that entire entity will never totally be an object of my jealousy, there can be no real locus of jealousy for me.

Jealousy has no ground at all but at the level of the body-mind-sense complex, no one except the Lord Himself seems to escape this special pain. For a *jñānin,* who knows the truth of himself, who therefore does not identify with the body-mind assemblage, there is no jealousy. A *jñānin* is not jealous because no second person exists. Thus, both the *jñānin* who knows himself to be the non-dual Brahman, and the Lord, who is not only the totality of the apparent but also knows the truth of Himself, know no jealousy; in fact, cannot be jealous. For others, jealousy exists and operates endlessly. Seeing themselves as separate entities, they see the world as filled with countless number of other entities that will daily present opportunities, real or fancied, for self-demeaning comparative judgements followed by the pain of *mātsarya.*

When analysed, it becomes very clear that jealousy is unfounded and unjustified. At the most elementary level of analysis, I can see that there is no absolute ranking of entities as 'subject to jealousy' or 'causing jealousy'. I am jealous of some; others are jealous of me. I can also see that there is no one who is an object of absolute jealousy. When I observe people closely, I invariably find things in them I do not want. Those who are jealous of me would also reject many things associated with me. Within the relative framework, jealousy is an illegitimate protest against the nature of apparent reality itself.

Jealousy, baseless as it is, nonetheless strikes at the heart of my deep dissatisfaction with myself, my desire to be different, to be full, to be complete. The undercurrent that always haunts me, the sense that I lack, the need for something to make me complete, feeds the fantasy of jealousy and gives it power to build up in my mind.

When I see the illegitimacy of jealousy, my mind will be inclined to *pratipakṣa-bhāvanā*. If the skill or grace or accomplishment of another pierces a barb of *mātsarya* in me, I deliberately bring this thought in mind; "I am happy to see someone with such excellence. I am happy to see the happiness of this person. I admire the person. I appreciate the person." By deliberate *pratipakṣa-bhāvanā* I nip the jealousy in the bud.

PRATIPAKṢA-BHĀVANĀ, A DAILY ACTION

Jealousy, resentment, selfishness and self condemnation are only few of the attitudes that can be handled by *pratipakṣa-bhāvanā*. Any attitude that is opposed to equanimity, accommodation, not hurting, absence of pride and similar values, can be neutralised by choosing to entertain the opposite point of view. This should be done daily. *Pratipakṣa-bhāvanā* is a daily act for the mind, just as bathing is for the body. *Pratipakṣa-bhāvanā,* at first, may seem false but as they are deliberately done, everyday, they will become real and spontaneous. A mind kept clean in this manner will be a quiet and alert mind. Such a mind is comfortable with itself, is ready to learn, and to be taught.

Sthairyam

Sthairyam is *niṣṭhā,* 'firmness' or 'steadiness'. Derived from the Sanskrit root '*sthā* - to stand' *sthairya* indicates constancy or perseverance. *Sthairya* is *karma-niṣṭhā, svadharma-niṣṭhā,* steadfastness in action, in one's duty. A steady effort on my part towards whatever goals I have committed to achieve or towards whatever duties my responsibilities impose upon me is *sthairya.*

When it comes to applying effort towards a goal, most of us find we are *ārambhaśūrāḥ,* heroes at the start. We begin very bravely, lions of resolution at first, but then the initial enthusiasm wanes. The energy of the heroic beginner dwindles when the total effort required becomes clear. We find some pretext to escape from the responsibility. Lack of steadfastness towards a commitment results in non-achievement of goals, which in turn builds up guilt of failure. *Sthairya* means there should be steady effort towards whatever we have committed to achieve until it is achieved, a steadiness that neither yields to laziness nor is disturbed by distraction.

In this context, where Lord Kṛṣṇa is talking about the values that make the mind ready to discover the truth of the self, *sthairya* refers to *niṣṭhā,* firmness, in seeking self-knowledge. When my commitment is to know the truth of myself, I need steadiness in the means, *sādhana-niṣṭhā,* to accomplish this goal. I must apply myself steadily to the secondary qualifications, such ascultivating certain attitudes, study of language, of the scriptures and similar pursuits that prepare my mind for self-knowledge.

The knowledge of the self is not a partial knowledge. It is not like the knowledge of a given discipline, but something total, the total content of all knowledge. For this goal, the goal in which all other goals resolve, total commitment is involved. In this total commitment, there must be *sthairya,* steadfastness.

Ātmavinigrahaḥ

Ātmavinigraha means mastery over the mind. The Sanskrit word *ātmā* basically is the name for whatever is referred to by the first person singular 'I'. In this capacity, *ātman* indicates many things which, depending upon the frame of reference, have the sense of 'I'. *Ātman* can be used for the physical body or it can refer to the vital functions of the body. Mind can be called *ātman* or sometimes *ātman* stands for the 'ego' sense of the mind, the *ahaṅkāra. Ātman* also is *saccidānanda,* the timeless, limitless awareness that is the truth of 'I'.

Less clearly but in a similar sense, in English, the pronoun 'I', when analysed refers to various functions and assemblages, as well as to the ultimate content of 'I-ness', depending upon the speaker's context. 'I am tired' is body-I. 'I am hungry' is a physiological-I. 'I know this', 'I am sad', 'I have decided to do this', are the various activities of the mind-I. 'I own it'; 'I did it', 'I enjoy it', are *ahaṅkāra*-I, the ego-I. The pronoun 'I' can mean, when the speaker knows the nature of himself, the "I am" of *saccidānanda,* the fullness that cannot be qualified. Here, in the context of Lord Kṛṣṇa's instruction to Arjuna, *ātman* refers to the mind, *antaḥkaraṇa*. *Vinigraha* means 'restraint' or 'curbing' which, in order to avoid any connotation of coercion or repression, is translated with reference to this value as 'mastery'.

What is mastery of the mind? Is it checking or controlling the grey matter, the cells of the brain? No, that which must be mastered is not the brain; what must be mastered is our ways of thinking. The mind is a colourful kaleidoscope of fanciful thoughts that come and go. Never constant, rarely still, subject to sudden starts and turns, capricious notions, the mind is whimsical by nature. However, I, the thinker, need not fulfil the fancies or yield to the caprices. Fancies and notions are many; that is the mind. But I am the sanctioning authority.

Even in relative terms the mind is not a definable entity, being only a collection of changing thoughts shaped by my ways of thinking. In general, the ways of thinking are of three types, impulsive, in which unexamined instinctive thoughts dominate, mechanical, in which prior conditioning is the dictator and thirdly, deliberate, wherein the evaluating function of my mind, *buddhi,* consciously examines the thoughts, accepts or dismisses them in accordance with my value structure.

There is a fourth way of thinking, spontaneous, in which my thoughts, without deliberation, conform to the highest universal values. Spontaneous thinking of this kind manifests at an absolute level only in one who has self-knowledge. At a relative level, spontaneous thinking reflects the degree to which universal values have become my personal and assimilated values. In essence, spontaneous thinking is complete *ātmavinigraha*. However, as a preparation for self-knowledge, initially we need to achieve relative mastery.

Ātmavinigraha, mastery over my ways of thinking, can be only relative since complete mastery requires knowledge of the self. It is only knowledge of the self that can completely destroy the hold of the likes and dislikes that compel and condition my ways of thinking. Thus, when Lord Kṛṣṇa tells Arjuna that *ātmavinigraha* is part of *jñāna,* preparatory for self-knowledge, this qualification must be taken as relative.

What is relative mastery? Complete mastery is characterised by spontaneity. If I am impulsive or conditioned, I am not a master. If I am deliberate, I am not a complete master. By being deliberate, I can be a relative master. Relative mastery is characterised by being alert and deliberate. I have relative mastery over my ways of thinking when I rationally examine my thoughts and either consciously accept or dismiss them. Relative mastery means both submitting all impulses to rational scrutiny and breaking any habit of lapsing into mechanical behaviour.

Śama, dama and *samādhāna* are Sanskrit terms often used to indicate different aspects of *ātmavinigraha*. *Śama* is discipline over thinking at the level where the thoughts arise, whereas, *dama* indicates choice exercised over thoughts and actions expressed at the level of the sense organ or organs of action. *Samādhāna* indicates *cittaikāgratā*, single pointedness of the mind, a way to describe the capacity of the mind to stay with a given line of thinking, a certain steadiness of thought of the mind. *Cittaikāgratā* is the art of applying the mind consistently to a given pursuit for a length of time.

The exercise of choice at the level of *śama* and *dama* establishes an abiding mind capable of *samādhāna*. The art of *samādhāna* or *cittaikāgratā* can then be learnt by beginning to apply the mind with a sharpened vigilance for distractions. *Ātmavinigraha* is a matter of alertness and awareness. If I am alert and conscious of what my mind is doing, I always have a choice over my ways of thinking. With choice, I can change. I can conform my behaviour to values. With choice, I can learn from mistakes. With choice, I can hold to commitments in the face of distraction. Choice requires alertness that makes possible relative mastery over my ways of thinking.

Indriyārtheṣu Vairāgyam

Indriya means sense organ and *artha* stands for object. *Vairāgya,* dispassion, comes from the word *rāga,* passion or desire joined to the negative prefix, *vi.* Thus, *indriyārtheṣu vairāgyam* means dispassion towards the objects of the sense organs or the absence of a compelling drive for worldly pleasures and possessions.

Rāga is more than just a fancy or preference; it is a craving for something. One who is free from such cravings is called a *vairāgin* and the state of his mind, *bhāva,* is called dispassion, *vairāgya.* What does dispassion mean? Does it mean putting a barrier between sense objects and me? Should I turn my head away, not look or listen when there is something that fascinates me? No, dispassion is not a state of inner suppression. It is a serene state of mind characterised by total objectivity towards the things of the world, the objects of the senses.

Dispassion is not suppression of desire. Dispassion and self-suppression are contradictory states of mind; they are mutually exclusive. Self-suppression is predicated on the presence of passion to be overpowered or crushed. In dispassion there is nothing there that requires suppression. No compelling desires command the mind of the *vairāgin*.

How can a mind be freed from compelling desires? How can I gain a dispassionate disposition? Dispassion is gained by clearly seeing objects for what they are; by seeing, without subjective distortion, how objects relate to me, to my happiness and welfare.

Basically, a human being seems to find himself or herself a wanting person. All my compelling desires turn upon this human sense of want. The common human experience is that I am not complete, I am lacking and I want to be a complete person. Seeing myself as incomplete, unfulfilled, inadequate, insecure, I try to bring completeness to myself by the pursuit of pleasure and the acquisition of things. I devote myself to two of the fundamental human pursuits, the struggle for *kāma* and that for *artha*. *Kāma* is the Sanskrit word for all forms of sense pleasure. *Kāma* indicates not just eating, but gourmet eating, not just drinking, but also drinking as a compelling pleasure. *Artha* stands for all that I think will bring me security in life—wealth, power, influence, fame and name.

As a human being, there will be no end to my longing and struggle for *artha* and *kāma,* so long as I feel both insecure and incomplete and think that *artha* and *kāma* have the capacity to provide security and completeness, and I will not be able to gain dispassion for sense objects, *indriyārtheṣu vairāgyam.* To become free from the compelling drive that is called *rāga,* the desire for things, *artha* and pleasures, *kāma,* I must analyse and discern that having a number of things does not make me secure nor does any amount of pleasure fill my sense of emptiness. I must discover that my struggle to fulfil my sense of want is endless. No accumulation of wealth is enough to silence the inner anxiety, no pleasure sufficient to bring lasting fulfilment.

Every gain, acquisition of any kind of wealth, also involves loss. No gain is ever absolute. Every such gain involves a concomitant loss, a loss through the expenditure of time and effort required; a loss through responsibility assumed; a loss through some other alternative abandoned. Gain involves loss. A lasting sense of security is never achieved through *artha*. When I analyse pleasure I find the same result. Human struggle for pleasure does not produce lasting contentment. I, like other human beings, live in a private, subjective world where I see objects as desirable, undesirable or neutral, neither desired nor undesired. When I observe reflectively, I find that what is desired by me is not desired by me at all times, at all places; nor is what I desire necessarily desired by other persons. What I desire, what brings me pleasure, is subject to constant change. Moments of pleasure require the concurrent availability of three factors, availability of the object of pleasure, availability of the appropriate effective instrument for enjoyment, and presence of the proper frame of mind to enjoy the object. Being dependent on these ever-changing factors, moments of pleasure are occasional and fleeting. Objects and instruments are bound by time; the mind is whimsical. It is subject to mood-change, discovering monotony in what was formerly desirable.

Analysis of pleasure shows that pleasure, like possessions, fails me in my effort to find fullness and completeness. Pleasure proves to be momentary and capricious while possessions, no matter how many, do not equate with security. My *rāga*, my passionate desire for possessions and pleasure, is based on my conviction that through the gain of *artha* and *kāma*, my sense of want will end. When I clearly see that is not the case, the best I can hope for in the aggregation of wealth is the exchange of one kind of anxiety for another. Moreover, the most I can claim from pleasure is a collection of fleeting moments, impossible to hold or predict. Hence, I am ready to discover in myself the state of *vairāgya*, not from self-denial but from an understanding that loosens the hold of *rāga* upon me. I see that objects, whether sought for pleasure or security, really cannot give me what I seek basically. If I wish to be dispassionate, I must know this fact very clearly. Objects are useful, but none of them can give me what I really want. I see that I cannot find complete or lasting security in wealth or power or fame, nor can I find lasting fullness in accumulated moments of pleasure.

When I do not place my security, my fullness, and my happiness in these things, I become more objective towards them. I treat them as objects, which I can assess for what they are rather than for what I subjectively expect from them. As simple objects rather than the answer to my most profound needs, they assume their proper position. I do not give them an extra value that, in reality, they do not have. I see money as money, not as a guarantee against insecurity. I see a house as a house, not as a source of happiness. I see land as land, not as an extension of myself through possession. I see these things as they are. When I see objects stripped of the subjective values that I have projected upon them, when I cease to look upon them as a source of happiness, I become objective. I become dispassionate. This is the mental state of *vairāgya*.

Vairāgya is an important value, one that must be understood correctly. Much nonsense is written about *vairāgya,* leading to confusion. *Vairāgya* is a state of mind brought about by understanding, not a state of mind compelled by a commitment to self-denial or deprivation. *Vairāgya* is not born out of fear or teeth-clenched effort of will but is born of sheer understanding. It is a knowledge produced by observation, inquiry and analysis. I question why and what I desire and what I achieve by fulfilling my desires. The understanding born of this analysis reduces the world to an objective fact for me; releases it from the tangle of my own subjectivity, the tangles of my likes and dislikes that bind me to situational happiness.

It is my subjective value for things that makes what is a simple object into an object of special distinction, an object peculiarly important to me. Such objects then bind me. It is because I bind myself, not because the object binds me. No house binds me; I am bound to the house because of the subjective value I place on it, a subjective value based upon my failure to understand its inability to deliver what I expect from it. Things do not catch and hold me; it is I who catch them. The handle is in myself, my subjective values based upon failure to understand the limitations of things to fulfil me. When I understand, the handle disappears and I see things as they are. This state of seeing, understanding, is called *indriyārtheṣu vairāgyam*, dispassion towards sense objects.

Anahaṅkāraḥ

Ahaṅkāra is a Sanskrit word that indicates the sense of concept of one's own individuality, the individualised I-sense expressed as 'I do', 'I own', 'I enjoy' and so on. '*An*' is a prefix which negates the meaning of the word it precedes. Therefore, *anahaṅkāra* means the absence of the sense of *ahaṅkāra*', freedom from an individualised 'I-identification'.

Total destruction, *nāśa* of *ahaṅkāra* is self-knowledge. Only the one who knows the truth of the self is completely free from *ahaṅkāra*, identification with an individualised 'I'. Lord Kṛṣṇa could not have intended the primary meaning of self-knowledge, total destruction, as the meaning of *anahaṅkāra*. Instead, the word has a relative meaning in which it is a preparatory means for knowledge.

What is meant by relative absence of *ahaṅkāra*? *Ahaṅkāra* is ego. How can you bring about relative absence of ego? By understanding what causes the presence of ego. Presence of ego is the result of sheer ignorance. Ego gains its status because I never think of examining its reality. The aggrandizement of ego comes about purely due to lack of thinking on my part. When I clearly, objectively examine the claims made by the ego, it cannot but deflate. The claim made by the ego will not hold up, either to knowledge or to ignorance or to power, possessions or accomplishments.

In a given lifetime, the essential characteristic of the individualised sense of I, in its infancy, is ignorance. Ignorance is the capital with which the 'I', ego begins life. Later, I maintain that capital and spend it very carefully throughout my life. Ignorance is not an ego inflator. Ignorance is not something to which I proudly lay claim. Knowledge, however, is a different matter. I gladly claim title to knowledge, although it is a spurious claim. Knowledge is not created by me, but only discovered in the wake of the removal of ignorance. Knowledge is always there; no one owns or creates knowledge. Hence, I cannot assign to the ego, a personal credit for the skill or speed in shedding ignorance.

When this individualised sense of 'I' came to manifest, it was endowed with certain kind of physical body, born into a particular set of circumstances or environment, both preset factors that condition the learning opportunities. Parents, teachers, neighbours, schools, and various experiences, contributed to the removal of my ignorance. *Ahaṅkāra* did not create the people or circumstances, yet claims the result.

Ahaṅkāra, ego, and *mānitva,* pride, are closely related, almost synonymous effects born of the same cause, ignorance of the relationship of the individualised sense of I with the world. We previously saw, when *mānitva* was examined, that pride in anything is a logical absurdity. Although, graced by free will, I have the power to choose my actions, I have no power over the actual result of the action chosen; the result I anticipate can never be more than a probability among possibilities. I do not produce the result. The result of any act of mine, occurs both as the product of materials that I have not authored as well as the outcome of many circumstances, past and present, known and unknown, which must operate in concert for the given result to occur.

If my strong skilful arm throws the winning pass in the final seconds of an American football game, the material and circumstantial factors that come together to produce this are too many for the final result to be a matter for personal pride. I am neither the creator of the football itself nor of my athletic body. Many people and experiences contributed to the development of the skill in the arm that threw the ball. I am not responsible for the clearing of the rainstorm so that the game did not have to be cancelled, or for the sharp earth tremor that occurred 60 seconds after my pass, since a minute earlier, my pass would have been spoiled. Nor can I claim credit for my colleague who caught the pass to convert the possibility into the winning points.

Pride and ego, when examined, become so silly that humility really cannot be considered a virtue. Humility is simply understanding the world, including myself, because I am part of the world, just as it is. When I understand things as they are, I will be neither proud nor will I be self-condemning. Self-condemnation also is an expression of the ego, *ahaṅkāra*.

We have already seen that self-condemnation is *āntara-aśauca,* an impurity in the mind, to be cleansed by the understanding that there is no locus for condemnation other than a particular thought.

In the correct understanding of myself, of my relationship to the world, there is no room for either pride or self-condemnation. I see the world that includes me, as it is. I see the world is filled with wonderful opportunities. Therefore, I make use of these opportunities as a source of learning. I make use of this vehicle, the body-mind and so on, to the best of my ability. It is my means to shed ignorance. I see that personal credit for anything is irrelevant and cannot be substantiated. I simply enjoy the world as a field for the discovery of knowledge, without pride, without egotism. This is the attitude of *anahaṅkāra*.

Janma-Mṛtyu-Jarā-Vyādhi-Duḥkha-Doṣānudarśanam

This long word, *janma-mṛtyu-jarā-vyādhi-duḥkha-doṣa-anu-darśanam,* is a Sanskrit compound noun that stands for a certain rigorously objective attitude towards life. *Anu,* the penultimate word of the compound, means repetitively, or again and again. *Anu* is prefixed to *darśanam,* a beautiful word that means 'seeing'. Seeing as in English also indicates knowing; when I see, I know. I see the solution means I know the solution.

What is the *anudarśanam,* the repeated seeing that Lord Kṛṣṇa is talking about? It is seeing the limitations, *doṣa,* in life itself, from birth to death. Life begins with birth, *janma.* Along with *janma* comes death, *mṛtyu,* the inseparable mirror-twin of birth. There is no birth that does not bring death along with it; everything that begins, ends. What is born has to die. The old man, death, always comes along with birth. While you are busy doing things, he is there patiently waiting. "All right, let him be busy" he says, but when he thinks you have played enough, he comes. *Janma* and *mṛtyu,* are but the opposite sides of a single coin.

In between *janma* and *mṛtyu* there are other *doṣa*s to see. These are old age, *jarā*, disease, *vyādhi* and so on. You may still be very young or perhaps strong and vigorous in your middle years but one thing you can count upon, if *mṛtyu* sufficiently spares you, *jarā* will creep in. The longer you elude *mṛtyu*, the more certainly a time will come when your hearing will grow dull; your vision will grow dim; your step will be unsteady; you may be uncomfortable while sitting; you may be uncomfortable while lying down. You will have problems—hearing problem, eating problem, digesting problem, thinking problem, remembering problem, sitting-standing-walking problem. What is this? It is old age, *jarā*, which is lurking around the corner.

"Well and good," you may say, "so death and old age are limitations, *doṣa*s, that come with birth, *janma*. I will try to remember them once in a while, but both are a long time away for me. I am young and healthy. There is a lot of life to enjoy before old age and death draw close to me."

Young you may be, but youth is no escape from the limitations of life. Two others, disease, *vyādhi* and pain, *duḥkha*, will introduce themselves to you in infancy, perhaps even before birth. Disease is something that goes with you all the time. Even before birth it is there. Sometimes it shows up, sometimes it does not, but it is always there, a shadow in your life. All may be bright and beautiful today. Three days from now you may be too sick to eat; too weak to move. You may be a champion athlete now only to be a chronic invalid with a lingering illness by this time next year. Disease can come any time, any place. It is not limited to a particular time or age.

Similarly, *duḥkha,* is a life-long companion. *Duḥkha* means all forms of pain, physical or mental, large or small, from the bite of a mosquito to grief over loss of a loved one. Pain, like disease, cannot be avoided. Careful as you may be, pain will catch you. A truck driving on the wayside of the street sends you to the hospital or, the earth grumbles and rumbles beneath your feet, shaking down the house to which you are so attached and giving you a dump on the head for good measure. This is called *duḥkha,* pain of various kinds that come in a variety of ways.

Pain or troubles coming from within are *ādhyātmika,* from the outside, *ādhibhāutika,* and from a heavenly source, *ādhidaivika*. *Ādhyātmika duḥkha*, internal pain, comprises the aches and pains and troubles of my individualised person. *Ādhibhautika duḥkha*, external pain, is made up of the problems the world around me, the smoke in the air, the blast of my neighbour's radio, the furnace that fails on a cold day and so on. *Ādhidaivika duḥkha* is the painful result of an event over which there is no control whatsoever, a tsunami, an earthquake or an erupting volcano.

Thus, we see the limitations, *doṣa*, in life. With birth, certain limitations come such as death, old age, disease and pain of all kinds. You cannot escape them. Therefore, bear in mind the nature of life. It is uncertain, painful and swiftly moving towards old age and death. Keep your mind on your purpose in life. Don't fritter it away. Remember time, *kāla*, is the devourer of the world, *kālo jagad-bhakṣakaḥ*.

Thus, the value, '*janma-mṛtyu-jarā-vyādhi-duḥkha-doṣa-anu-darśanam*', that Lord Kṛṣṇa teaches Arjuna, is an important value. It is not negative but simply factual. Its purpose is to direct your attention to the need to see the life objectively, just as it is, so that you will be able to make use of the time that is available in your hands right now. Available time is precious time. Make use of it, consciously. Consciously use your time for your activities and pursuits. Work. Play. Sleep. Just eating, relaxing, walking—one day you will find time has passed over you and suddenly you are old. If you make use of time consciously, you are a master, swami, of time.

Asaktiḥ

Sakti means clinging attachment to things. This attitude of 'holding fast' to things underlies the notion of ownership. *Asakti* means the absence of the attitude of ownership, absence of the attitude that anything peculiarly belongs to me. Ownership is notional; possession is factual. *Asakti* is reduction of all false relationships involving claims of ownership to factual relationships.

Analysis shows that no claim to ownership can survive close scrutiny. Nothing is really mine. I cannot claim exclusive, permanent title to anything, to land, to knowledge, to people, to things, or even to my own body-mind unit. When I analyse anything that I think I own, I find that there is nothing to own; there is only something to possess. Take the house where I live. That I possess this house is a fact. Physically I am present there in person and I make use of the property. But whether or not I am the owner of the house depends not upon the physical fact of my presence but upon a consensus of notions about my relationship to the particular property.

To see how notional ownership is, let us consider this situation. A friend of yours, who owns a nice house with a large compound, decides to go to the United States for better career opportunities. He asks you to 'house-sit'for him while he is gone. You will live in the house and protect it from vandals. He will not charge you rent, but you are expected to maintain and pay the insurance and taxes while you live there. Since this is a very good deal for such a fine house you quickly accept. Your friend, who does very well in the States, from year to year, postpones returning home to reclaim his property. One day while you are at work you receive an overseas telephone call from your friend. He is jubilant. He has struck it rich in a mining syndicate and is settling abroad permanently. In a magnanimous gesture, he is making gift of the house to you. He has already instructed his lawyer to prepare the deed.

That evening when you go home, nothing physical, nothing tangible, will have changed about you and the house. You still live there as you have for the past five years. You intend to continue living there. You have been paying for the maintenance, taxes and insurance. You will continue to do so. You don't intend to sell the house. There has been no material change, but now you are the legal owner of the house, and your whole attitude towards it has changed. You call a real estate broker to see how much it is worth. You decide to put up a fence. You inquire about the zoning laws. You go across the street to get a better perspective and look at the house with a proprietary feeling. Nothing has really changed, except the legal position. It is now your house. You now consider yourself the owner that gives that property a special hold upon you.

That ownership is purely notional, and is even more clearly seen in the case of flats or modern condominiums. A few years ago a young friend told me that he had bought a new place in Mumbai, which he invited me to see. When we arrived at his house, I found myself looking at a seven-storey structure. Since this young man has a relatively modest position I was surprised.

"You bought this?" I asked.

"Not all of it," he laughed, "I own a flat on the third floor."

So we went to the third floor and he ushered me in, saying, "This is mine. This is the flat I own."

This was the first time I had heard of such an arrangement, so I was still puzzled.

"Do you own the land?" I asked.

"No," he said, and explained that a co-operative management society owned the land. All he owned was one rather small flat, two rooms and a kitchen.

So I asked, "What is it you own of this flat? Do you own the floor?"

"No. My floor is the ceiling of the fellow downstairs."

"Do you own the ceiling?"

"No, the ceiling is the floor for the family upstairs."

"How about the walls?"

"Well, the inner walls are shared with other flats. The outer wall, of course, belongs to the whole building as part of its structural support."

"So what do you own?"

"Well, Swamiji, I own the space."

You can see the nature of ownership. A claim of ownership is always connected with something over which at the most I can assert is a temporary possession or control. Even my right to sell that which I own is a possessing right, nothing more. I can transfer my possession or control of something to another for which I receive certain money. This is only a transfer of possession. For me to claim an ownership, that is factually more than a temporary possession, I would have to be the sole, absolute author of the owned object. Otherwise many before me as well as those who come after me will also be able to claim rights in the object, reducing my factual status to its temporary possessor or controller.

As we have seen before, I cannot claim to be the sole author of anything. I did not create the land on which my house stands. I did not make the materials that went into the house. Fire and water were needed. The work of many other people went into the house—masons, carpenters, electricians, plumbers and so on. Conformity to certain physical laws, not my creation, made possible the assurance that the walls will stand.

Thus, my house, which is made up of the materials available in an existent creation, as assembled by or in accordance with the knowledge of countless human beings unknown to me, some long dead, is simply an aggregate structure available for my temporary possession and control.

That is well and good, you may say, for a tangible object external to me, like a house, but there is something uniquely and specially mine, for which I certainly can claim factual ownership. That unique thing is my own body. Who else can claim my body?

Many others can make claims over any given body. The mother can say, "I bore this body. It is flesh of my flesh. It is mine, not separate from me." "No," says the father. "I am the instrumental cause, *nimitta kāraṇa*, of this body. I was involved in its creation. Not only did I provide all the food necessary for this body to grow but the clothes and shelter also to protect it."

The society, the community has a claim to the body. Collectively the efforts of many have made available the things necessary for this body to be nurtured and have provided a society in which it can live. A spouse can say, “This body belongs to me, a partner in marriage. We are two halves of a single marriage unit. I too have a claim.” A child born to the marriage also will assert a claim, “This body has a duty to me, to stay alive and perform work, so I will be cared for while my body grows up.”

It is endless—the people, the creatures, the materials and substances that can claim rights to this body: the family, the employer, the State; water, space, fire, air, goats, cows, sheep, grains, grass, fruits, vegetables, earth and sun, not to mention worms, mosquitoes, bugs and bacteria. The vulture says, “Some day soon that body is going to be my dinner.” “Oh, no,” says the virus, “for generations it has been my home.”

Thus, even for my own body, I am only a managing trustee, nothing more than that. I am the in-dweller of this body. It is in my possession. As possessor I can say, my body, but only in terms of possession, definitely not in terms of ownership. Even the laws of the State recognise that bodies are entrusted. State laws prohibit suicide, reflecting the recognition that a body is a thing entrusted to the possession of a person but which the person has no right to kill. He has the right to maintain it but not to destroy it, a possessive right only to make use of it.

An attitude of possession rather than an attitude of ownership towards anything is a relief whether it is towards house, money or one's own body. An attitude of possession puts the relationship with the thing claimed in factual perspective that promotes dispassion and objectivity. The relationship is seen for what it is, non-exclusive, impermanent but at the same time a presently existing entrustment of possession to be enjoyed and properly maintained. This is the right attitude towards my mind, towards any wealth I may have, towards the people around me, to all of them I relate with *asakti,* without a clinging attachment, without an attitude of ownership. I recognise ownership as purely notional; that possession alone is a fact. I reduce all my false notional ownership, relationships to factual relationships.

Asakti, non-attachment in the sense of seeing my relationship to things objectively, is another example of dispassion, *vairāgya*. Previously, in *indriyārtheṣu vairāgyam* we saw dispassion towards sense objects being highlighted. I gain a dispassion towards sense objects when I recognise that sense objects do not have the capacity to produce lasting happiness or security. In *asakti* the dispassion highlighted is the relationship between me and objects. It is the dispassion I discover when I see clearly that there can be no valid nor lasting attachment to anything; that is, there is no valid ownership of anything.

ANABHIṢVAṄGAḤ PUTRA-DĀRA-GṚHĀDIṢU

Abhiṣvaṅga is the kind of intense attachment or affection you feel for what is particularly beloved such as a son, *putra*, wife, *dārā*, or house, *gṛha* and so on, *ādi*, all other similar people and things dear to you. *Abhiṣvaṅga* can be defined as *atisneha*. *Sneha* has the literal meaning of viscous and the figurative meaning of affection. *Ati* means excessive. So *abhiṣvaṅga* is *atisneha*, an excessive affection. The particle '*an*' added makes the word negative. So here *anabhiṣvaṅga* means the absence of excessive attachment for those people or things that are generally considered very dear, *putra-dāra-gṛhādi*.

Essentially, *anabhiṣvaṅga*, here, in the sense of a value, means dispassionate caring. Lord Kṛṣṇa is not counselling abandonment of care or affection for family but is calling for objectivity in that caring. In the discussion of the attitude of *asakti*, absence of the notion of ownership, we saw that we cannot have a special, total claim on any person or thing. In the understanding born of *asakti*, freedom from ownership, we will have *anabhiṣvaṇga,* lack of excessive attachment towards family. However, it does not mean lack of care; it means care and affection with dispassion.

Nityaṁ Samacittatvam Iṣṭāniṣṭopapattiṣu

Sama-cittatvam iṣṭāniṣṭopapattiṣu simply means that we accept with 'sameness of mind' the results we like as well as the results we do not like. *Sama* means equal. *Cittatvam* means state of mind. *Iṣṭāniṣṭopapattiṣu* means the occurrence of something considered desirable or undesirable.

Here, Lord Kṛṣṇa is telling Arjuna, always, *nityam*, maintain the sameness of mind, *sama-cittatvam*, in the wake of likes or dislikes. Do not be elated over getting what you want nor be dejected when you get what you do not want. Accept results as they come, factually. If an accident occurs, with sameness of mind, assess the situation and do what is required. If some venture fails, look at the facts, learn from them and do whatever is now needed. View all situations, as they occur, factually, with a mind unshaken by emotional intensity, a mind that calmly decides what is to be done and directs the doing of it.

When something happens that you like, do not get elated. A mind that becomes ecstatic when it gets what it thinks it wants will also hit the bottom when loss or failure occurs. *Sama-cittatva* is the state of mind that does not swing between elation and depression, but remains in equilibrium regardless of the situation—successful, unsuccessful, joyful, sorrowful, conducive, non-conducive and so on.

When I face every situation with a mind that neither gets elated nor depressed, I will be objective. The attitude of *sama-cittatva* is another example of reducing subjective response to factual acceptance. More often than not, we resist accepting facts. When we refuse to accept facts, facts become problems. When we hear unpleasant or sad news, our first response usually is outright rejection of the facts or to delay acceptance.

The following response, attributed to a great stoic philosopher upon hearing tragic news, illustrates reduction of facts to facts.

The philosopher who was waiting for the news of the safe arrival of a large sailing ship carrying his wife and children and all his wealth, answered a knock on his door and found a breathless messenger who announced, " Sir, the ship carrying your family and wealth has sunk!"

"What?"

"The ship has sunk!"

"So what?"

"Sir, you have lost all your wealth."

"What?"

"Your fortune is gone."

"So what?"

"Sir, nothing was salvaged; you are penniless!"

"What?"

"You are a pauper!"

"So what?"

"Sir, no one survived. You have lost your wife and children."

"What?"

"You are a childless widower."

"So what?"

When the philosopher each time said "What?" it was neither because he had not heard the words nor because he failed to understand the sentence. He had heard and he had understood, but he said "What?" because at first he refused to accept it. Since it was not acceptable, he said, "What?" not to the messenger, really, but to himself. It was his initial refusal to accept the particular fact that each time made him first say, "What?" But, being a philosopher, he did not hang on to non-acceptance.

"The ship is sunk. So what? There is nothing I can do about it. I am a pauper. Well, so what? I am penniless. I made money and lost it. Now I'll work to make it again. My wife and children are gone. Grief and despair won't bring them back. They are gone. That is a sad fact. I assimilate the facts and do what is required of me under the circumstances."

There are pleasant facts and unpleasant facts. There are comfortable facts and uncomfortable facts and all the time the facts keep changing, now pleasant, now not so pleasant; now comfortable, now uncomfortable. The weather is too hot; the weather is just right; the weather is too cold. I feel on top of the world; I've come down with the flu. Each day brings facts of all kinds. My job is to greet all facts with sameness of mind. I accept and enjoy the comfortable facts for what they are, the facts of the moment. Similarly, I accept without reaction the uncomfortable facts for what they are. I simply do whatever the situation calls for. If I can make an uncomfortable fact more comfortable, I do so. If I cannot, I accept and do whatever is required.

The factual response is the approach to situations of a truly practical person. One is most practical when one sees situations objectively. This is real human strength. Human strength is not found in powerful miracles but in the quiet mind of the one who faces situations as they are. Such a one is a strong person. Human weakness is the inability to accept situations, to face facts. Human strength is the strength of reducing situations to simple facts.

When I strip away all my subjective projections from the facts of each situation, I will have sameness of mind in every situation. It is not the fact but my like or dislike projected onto the fact that causes my mind to react. As I reduce situations to facts without projecting my emotional reactions upon them, my mind assumes a poise that makes it easier to appreciate the vision of Vedanta. A relatively poised mind—one not muddled by projections upon it and external situations—is necessary to appreciate the teaching of Vedanta that deals with the nature of facts.

Vedanta reveals the reality of the facts of the objective world to be apparent, *mithyā*. However, for the mind to be ready to see the 'apparent-ness' of the world, to be ready to discover that it is seeking non-objectifiable, non-negatable reality, I have to reduce my projections with reference to the objective reality. When I project upon the facts of the objective world, my own subjective reality based upon my likes and dislikes, I am too muddled to see the truth found in the teaching of Vedanta. The teaching distinguishes the apparently real and unfolds the nature of reality.

A mind that is ready for the teaching of Vedanta is a mind that sees facts objectively, which does not convert a fact into a subjective problem but meets each situation with sameness of attitude, with a mental poise free from complaint. Such a mind, without subjective reaction, calmly determines what needs to be done in a particular situation.

Mayi Ananya-Yogena Bhaktiḥ Avyabhicāriṇī

This entire line, *mayi ananyayogena bhaktiḥ avyabhicāriṇī,* expresses the value of steadfast devotion to the Lord, devotion characterised by non-separateness from Him. Lord Kṛṣṇa, identifying himself as the Lord, describes the value, unswerving, *avyabhicāriṇī,* devotion, *bhaktiḥ,* by not combining with any other, *ananya-yogena,* in me, *mayi.* It refers to a steady, unswerving devotion, due to the recognition of my non-separateness from the Lord.

Non-separateness from the Lord can be seen in two ways. Either, non-separateness, *ananya-yoga,* means that the Lord is not separate from me. This is a view that comes when I know the truth of the Lord, of myself, and the creation. From this knowledge I can see that the Lord is never away from me. He is I; I am never away from the Lord; I am indeed non-separate from Him. Or, we can also say that the non-separateness is in terms of seeing the Lord as my refuge. For me there is no refuge other than Parameśvara, *parameśvarād anyaḥ mama śaraṇaṁ nāsti.* The Lord is everything; He is my security. He is the source of my inspiration.

By His laws come the results of my acts. He is the giver of the fruits of all actions, *karma-phala-dātā*.

Devotion based on the second way of looking at the Lord is very helpful in preparing my mind for self-knowledge in which I can see my total non-separateness from Him. It is through devotion to the Lord as the one who gives the results of action, that I can maintain that poise of mind called *sama-cittatva* described in the last value. There it was said that *sama-cittatva,* sameness of mind in the face of desirable or undesirable results, is made possible by reducing all situations to facts. Easy to say, but how do I bring about a factual attitude towards all that comes my way? This factual attitude, *sama-cittatva,* will come when I view all results as coming to me directly from the hands of the Lord.

Being human, my behaviour is not tightly pre-programmed by my instincts. I have been given the freedom of choice over actions. But the results of my actions are not something that I can choose. The results come from the Lord. I can choose to act, but once I have acted, I have no further choice. I cannot prevent the result from occurring, once the act is done, and that result may or may not be the result I expected or wanted.

The result of any action is always appropriate to the action, that is, the result is in accordance with the laws of the Lord, but I do not know all of those laws. Many laws shape the result, known laws, unknown laws, visible laws, invisible laws, while I have no knowledge or control over all the factors involved in producing a result. The actual result is always taken care of by the interplay of all the appropriate natural laws of the creation. Therefore, all results really come from the creator, the Lord.

When I view the results, from my own actions or from the actions of others, as coming from the Lord, I can have sameness of mind towards the results. Whatever happens, I will see it as a blessing, *prasāda*, given to me from the Lord's hand. *Prasāda* distributed from the altar is always acceptable, whatever it may be. I don't question it, because it comes from the Lord. I accept the Lord as the giver of the fruits of all actions. He never fails nor do His laws ever fail. Therefore, towards the operation of His laws I have an attitude of *prasāda*. This graceful acceptance of whatever comes to me from the Lord is called *prasāda-buddhi.* There is no regret; there is no failure; there is no elation; there is no depression. The attitude is simply graceful acceptance.

The graceful acceptance of all results brings sameness of the mind, *nityaṁ sama-cittatvam,* in the face of the desirable or the undesirable. Thus *nityaṁ sama-cittatvam* is the result of the more basic attitude of *prasāda-buddhi* which itself is grounded in a steadfast devotion to the Lord, seeing the Lord as the giver of the results of all actions.

The Lord says, "If there is unswerving devotion to me, *mayi ananyayogena avyabhicāriṇī bhaktiḥ,* seeing nothing other than me as the giver of results, naturally there will be sameness of mind, *nityaṁ sama-cittatvam iṣṭāniṣṭopapattiṣu,* for favourable and unfavourable results." This kind of devotion frees one from any kind of reaction. One simply sees things just as they are, as simple facts. Facts become problems only because I refuse to accept them; I refuse to accept facts because I had wanted them to be different. But if and when the facts arrive, when expectation turns into result, I take that result as *prasāda*; there will be no refusal of acceptance.

When we accept facts we can learn from them. Experience is a good teacher for the person with a mind clear of reactions, a mind attentive and available to be taught. However, since there is a reaction to facts, a resistance comes without sanction of will or wisdom. When my attitude towards facts is built upon whether I like them or not, I will always be subject to mindless reactions in which all my wisdom and mental poise vanish. I cannot programme the laws of creation to tailor the ever-changing situations to the measure of my shifting likes and dislikes. I can only, through devotion to the creator, gracefully accept situations with an attitude of interest and wonder at the environment provided by His hand for my cheerful discharge of duty and, perhaps in some cases, for some learning on my part for wiser action in the future.

When I have the attitude of non-separate devotion, *ananya-yogena bhaktiḥ,* towards the Lord, my standpoint towards myself, towards my actions and the results that come, will be a factual attitude. I will see that as a human being enjoying freewill, I can choose to act or not to act, but the results of my actions are not subject to my choice. This understanding will free me to review the results factually and choose further actions rationally.

However, when my attitude is one of thinking that I am the cause of the results of my actions, and that the acceptability of the results of my actions is determined by what I like and what I dislike, I will have a frame of mind that leads to responding to the world with reaction and not action. A mind in the grip of reactions loses its freedom of will to act.

A reaction to a situation is an automatic response not preceded by a thoughtful decision. Automatic responses occur sometimes from a thoughtless surrender to impulses, but more often a reaction is born of mental habits based on likes and dislikes. When I always respond to a situation in a manner determined by my likes and dislikes, there would be consistent reaction. My responses will be mechanical. I will have no control over them. When my actions are really reactions, my mind will be troubled, experience will not teach me. Conflicts between thought and deed will bother me; painful emotions will build up; mood will be my master.

A mind graced by devotion which sees the Lord as the giver of all the results of action will have few reactions because it knows that human freedom of will is given to choose actions not their results. These come from the Lord in accordance with His laws. Moreover, because results come from Him, there is never a wrong result or a result that one does not accept. One accepts, cheerfully, with even mind, what comes from His hand.

Such a mind, free from reactions is quiet and receptive. It can deal with negative emotions and is master over its mood. Objective and serene, a mind such as this is ready to discover the fact of *ananya-yoga,* the fact of one's non-separateness from the Lord and creation.

Vivikta-Deśa-Sevitvam

Vivikta-deśa-sevitva is love for a quiet place, for seclusion. *Deśa* is place. *Vivikta* means separate or solitary, and *sevitva* is to inhabit or resort to. So, *vivikta-deśa-sevitva* is a value for resorting to a secluded place.

Why should love for spending time in a solitary place be listed as a value? It is not the isolation of the place that makes the value, but what is valuable is the kind of mind that is happy in such place. A mind that is quiet and appreciates solitude is a mind that has a love for being with itself. This is a beautiful attitude that is not found very often in our society. We are a society of people bent on escaping from ourselves. We try to escape because we are not satisfied with ourselves. We see ourselves as not being the way we would like to be. Therefore, we keep the mind busy so there is no time, place or quiet in which we can be with ourselves. Even on the telephone, if there must be a waiting period, music will often be provided so the mind can be occupied.

We travel, from beach to mountain, sand to snow, and back again, to escape from ourselves.

Wanderlust is a good expression for this urge to travel. For the stay-at-home, amusement parks, movies, television, sporting events, magazines, newspapers, parties become the means for escape. It is not that there is anything wrong with travel or recreation; the problem is the need for escape. For some the avenue of escape may be drugs or gambling or drinking. Whether harmful or seemingly benign, the need to escape betrays reluctance on one's part to face oneself.

You can tell that activities have become an escape for you when, without the activity, you feel lost, sad, or incomplete. The occupation that leaves you feeling incomplete, when you cannot have it, has become an escape. A given activity by itself is neither an escape nor a non-escape. It is the reason behind the activity that makes it an escape or not. A happy person will sing because he has nothing else to do; that is not escape. But the escaping person also will sing because there is something he cannot face, and singing occupies his mind so he does not have to look at it. Singing or listening to music can be either an escape or a non-escape. When people become agitated, if they can sing, you will find they will begin whistling, humming or singing because they want to shake off certain thoughts. In fact, what they want to shake off is themselves, their reactions to an unwelcome thought. They think of some sad event or some mistake they have committed, then, immediately, a whistle will start or a song will come out. This is not the song of a happy person but the song of escape.

This tendency of the mind to want to escape is a universal thing. Everywhere in the world, the human mind is the same. Whether Indian or American or European, the basic tendencies in minds will be the same. Cultural differences are found only in the response to these basic, universal tendencies. From culture to culture the avenues of escape will be different, determined by the nature of the society in which one finds oneself. Social factors will determine the way of escape. But the desire of the mind to escape is a universal thing.

A person who enjoys being with himself in quietude is not a sad person. He is a simple, quiet, contemplative person. To be contemplative means to be able to face yourself happily. If you cannot face yourself happily, the mind will always require an escape. An escape is an occupation that engages the attention of the mind so that it does not have to be with itself.

For the one who wants self-knowledge, it is very important to have a value for being with oneself, for quietude. Lord Kṛṣṇa mentions this value *vivikta-deśa-sevitva* more than once in his counsel to Arjuna. In chapter vi, verse 10, of the *Gītā*, talking about meditation, Lord Kṛṣṇa tells Arjuna:

> *Yogī yuñjīta satatam ātmānaṁ rahasi sthitaḥ, ekākī...*
>
> The *yogin* should dwell constantly on the self, established in solitude, alone...

I learn to be with myself by willingly moving to a quiet place where I take stock of myself and learn to love and accept myself. When you have the habit of repairing to a quiet place, you are learning to be with yourself. When you have learned to be with yourself, you have come to terms with yourself. Clear knowledge of yourself, is now possible.

Aratiḥ Jana-Saṁsadi

Rati means love for something or inclination towards it. Adding '*a*' to *rati* makes the word indicate a lack of inclination towards something. *Jana* stands for people and *saṁsadi* means in an assembly or collection. So, this value means a lack of craving for company, not revelling in company, not courting company.

This is not a value that calls for hatred of company. Company is not bad. It is not that one should dislike being around people. If the people are there, fine, be happy in their presence. But know that you do not require people to be happy.

Love of quietude, *vivikta-deśa-sevitva,* in which one is happily with oneself, and not longing company, *aratiḥ jana-saṁsadi,* are companion values. They complement each other. It is not that a quiet place in and of itself is intrinsically something good, or that the presence of company is something bad, but the values are for a happy, non-escaping mind that loves being with itself. Such a mind is happy with itself in quietude, does not run after escape; neither revels in nor hates company. These are two beautiful attitudes. With these values, I will never need to seek escape from being with myself, nor will I be disturbed either by the presence or absence of people. I will have composure whether I am with people or without them.

It is important to see the basis of these attitudes, to see through the values to the value underneath them. *Aratiḥ jana-saṁsadi* is not a value for avoiding people; nor is *vivikta-deśa-sevitva* a value for seeking quietude because one cannot stand people. Someone who seeks seclusion out of hatred of people is not expressing these values. Such a person is afraid of people, and fear of people is not a desirable thing in life. Equally, the other extreme, courting the company of people all the time to escape from oneself, is not any more desirable than the fear of people.

The attitude that is proper is not hatred of people but a simple love of quietude, because I love to be with myself and therefore do not court company. This attitude establishes the right frame for a contemplative mind, for a mind given to inquiry, *vicāra*. Inquiry here means inquiry into the basic, profound questions about myself: Who am I? What is this creation? Who is God? What is the relationship between God, the creation and me?

Inquiry into these subtle questions requires special sensitivity of the mind, sensitivity beyond what is needed to inquire into the functioning or description of tangible object or processes. Inquiry into something tangible, how to make bread, or even the grammar of a language, is aided by having changing objects to see, to watch; one can see the modifications, *vikāra* taking place upon things, whether in a pan of dough or upon the stems of nouns and verbs.

However, when the *vicāra* is inquiry into the self, we are dealing with something that, although fundamental, is not tangible. The self is not a tangible object that lends itself to trial and error methods, checked by gross perceptions. The knowledge of the self must be seen as a whole. To appreciate the knowledge of the self, to see the self for the non-objectifiable wholeness that it is, requires a mind that is contemplative and sensitive.

However, the sensitivity does not imply getting hurt at every turn but it should be backed by healthy attitude and objectivity. Values come when I thoroughly understand my relationship to people, places and things around me. In a factual understanding, those situations, attitudes or events, which I consider hurtful, lose their significance for me and thereby their sting. Pride and pretence, which court hurt, drop away from me; non-harmfulness and accommodation, which soften hurt, become natural for me.

The mind that does not get hurt is an undisturbed, non-reacting, fresh, simple and a contemplative mind that can appreciate the whole as it unfolds in the teaching of self-knowledge. Resorting to a quiet place, *vivikta-deśa-sevitva*, and absence of the need for company, *aratiḥ jana-saṁsadi*, are attitudes that establish such a contemplative mind, a mind ready for a contemplative life centred on self-knowledge.

Tattva-Jñānārtha-Darśanam

Although this is the last value in the order given by Lord Kṛṣṇa, it will be considered next. The value, '*adhyātma-jñāna-nityatva*' will be discussed last. Consideration in this reversed order makes possible a more logical analysis because when the value '*tattva-jñānārtha-darśana*' is assimilated, expression of the value, '*adhyātma-jñāna-nityatva*' becomes very natural.

Tattva means truth, truth in the sense of the irreducible reality of anything and everything. *Jñāna* as used here in the compound *tattva-jñāna* is self-knowledge. *Artha* means purpose or an end in the sense of a goal. *Darśana* is sight or vision. So *tattva-jñānārtha-darśana* is keeping in view the purpose of the knowledge of truth. Knowledge of truth, *tattva-jñāna,* is the thing-to-be-known, *jñeya,* in life for which the values, indicated earlier by the word, '*jñāna*', prepare the mind.

So, what is the basic thing to be known in life? The basic knowledge to be discovered in life is the knowledge of what is, such as what is real, what is fundamental. What is sought is the knowledge of the truth, or the fundamental nature of oneself, the creation and the creator. This knowledge of the truth of what is, the truth of everything, is the meaning of *tattva-jñāna*. The basic knowledge of the truth can also be called the knowledge of self, *ātma-jñāna*, because, upon inquiry, the irreducible reality of oneself turns out to be not different from the irreducible reality of God and creation. In fact, this value can be described as not losing sight of self-knowledge as one's primary goal, having an overwhelming value for that goal, so that it does not become eclipsed by other goals but remains always in one's mind as the primary purpose in life, the recognised end behind all other ends that may be sought.

What is the purpose of self-knowledge?

To discover within oneself an overwhelming value for keeping in view the goal of self-knowledge, one needs to know what does one gain from self-knowledge? What is the purpose served by self-knowledge?

All human purposefulness can be classified under four headings. The collective Sanskrit name for these four headings is *puruṣārtha,* from *puruṣa,* human being, and *artha,* purpose, that for which a human being longs and struggles. They are *dharma, artha, kāma,* and *mokṣa.*

The four-fold pursuit in a human life

Dharma, ethical standards, refers to the goal of conforming one's behaviour to scripture-sanctioned ethical norms in order to obtain merit or avoid demerit in this life or the next. Alternately, for the one who is not an adherent to any particular scriptural sanctions, it means simply the universal set of ethical standards mandated by human free will and shaped by one's wish to be treated in a certain manner by one's fellow human beings.

Artha, security, refers to the goal of acquiring the things that one thinks will make one secure, such as money, property, possessions, power, influence, name and fame.

Kāma, pleasures, is the goal of enjoying the varieties of pleasures life affords, such as physical comforts, sensory delights, and mind-pleasing escapes.

Mokṣa, liberation, is the goal of discovering freedom from the hands of time; freedom from change, age, death, grief, and loss; escape from a never-ending sense of inadequacy and incompleteness from all forms of limitation, the desire to be rid of desire itself.

Looked at from the standpoint of the fourfold pursuit, self-knowledge, *ātma-jñāna,* which is synonymous with knowledge of truth, *tattva jñāna,* does not fit into any of the first three categories. Self-knowledge neither is mandated by scripture for the sake of obtaining merit, *puṇya,* nor for the avoidance of demerit, *pāpa,* nor is it a commonsense ethical standard serving the interest of free-willed, self-conscious beings interacting with one another. Therefore, the purpose of self-knowledge is not to serve scriptural or common sense ethics, *dharma.*

Moreover, self-knowledge does not result in the gain of either securities, *artha* or pleasures, *kāma.* Knowledge does not produce possessions or pleasures. Actions, efforts are required to gain securities or pleasures. Particular knowledge may be needed or useful as an aid to the effort required for a given security or pleasure but the purpose itself is fulfilled by the effort, not by the knowledge. Knowledge shapes the effort; the effort does the job. There is no knowledge, not even the knowledge of truth that can produce *artha* or *kāma.*

Where then, does self-knowledge belong? There is only one category left and that is liberation, *mokṣa*, which is, in fact, where *ātma-jñāna* fits. Self-knowledge serves the purpose of *mokṣa*. The value *tattva-jñānārtha-darśana* means keeping in sight the goal of *mokṣa*, which is complete freedom from the human sense of limitation, incompleteness, and inadequacy. The state of mind of the person, who constantly keeps in view *mokṣa*, is called *mumukṣutva*; the seeker of liberation is called a *mumukṣu*.

Thus, the value of *tattva-jñānārtha-darśana* can also be called the value of *mumukṣutva*, the value for the human freedom. A *mumukṣu* never loses sight of the freedom he seeks, nor does he compromise or settle for a lesser thing. Like a salmon swimming out of the ocean back into the river from which it came, where, against all odds, it battles the current in its single-pointed drive back to its place of origin, so too, does the *mumukṣu* seek freedom, a freedom that is discovered in the knowledge of the truth of one's origin.

Any human seeking is, basically, a search for liberation. However, most people seek in places where liberation is not available. The usual seekers have not singled out that freedom itself is the fundamental human end, but instead, keep their vision sighted on a house, a job, a vacation, a marriage or whatever represents a step toward completeness for them. Among these usual strugglers, some single out *mokṣa* as their goal when they have discovered that achievements do not bring lasting satisfaction and, perhaps, have chanced upon some book or other writing that discusses liberation.

Whatever the source, be it a book, a travelling swami, an informed friend, when the information about *mokṣa* hits ready ears, the search for information about the means to *mokṣa* begins. This search itself can lead a seeker over a lot of ground from *yoga* to therapy, from *guru* to *guru*, in a process of negation and natural selection until the goal of *mokṣa* gains definition and direction; and the means to it, which is knowledge alone, becomes clear.

Knowledge is the only means to freedom

Why is knowledge the only means to freedom, *mokṣa*? It is because the freedom sought is limitlessness itself, that choiceless human goal underlying all other human struggles for limited ends. Limitlessness is not something that can be created or produced. If limitlessness exists, it is an ever-existent fact to be discovered. If my essential nature is that of a limited being, I can never become limitless. Limitlessness, by definition, can never be the end product of a process of becoming. An endless series of limited things will not constitute limitlessness. Limited means cannot produce limitlessness. Limitlessness either is or it is not.

Therefore, if I am by essential nature bound, there can be no *mokṣa* for me; I can never be absolutely liberated. Often, as I look at the world around me and at myself, I judge myself to be bound, limited, inadequate, and sorrow-prone. At the same time, there is within me that love for freedom that in occasional moments of joy or insight seems to be fulfilled as fact, contradicting all my experiences of inadequacy. Thus, even though my usual experience is that of being limited, on the basis of my innate need to be free, backed by intimations that freedom may be my nature, I am led to search for knowledge of the truth of myself to discover whether or not I am that being I want to be. If the freedom I seek is an accomplished fact, my failure to appreciate that fact can only be due to ignorance; and if my only problem is one of ignorance, search for liberation becomes a search for the knowledge that will dispel the ignorance that keeps me from knowing myself as I am.

A search for *mokṣa,* which has become a search for knowledge, is an informed *mumukṣutva,* which is a quest for freedom characterised by recognition of the underlying basic human need to be free. One becomes an informed seeker of freedom by examining one's own efforts, experiences, being limited, do not produce lasting freedom, and by the comprehension that it is through knowledge and knowledge alone that one does gain freedom. It is the desire for freedom, *mumukṣutva,* which has matured into a desire to know, *jijñāsā,* which indicates a state of mind bent on inquiry for the sake of knowledge.

What knowledge does the *mumukṣu* seek? He or she seeks the knowledge of the truth of oneself, *ātma-jñana,* which can also be called the knowledge of truth, *tattva-jñāna. Tattva-jñānārtha-darśana* simply is a value for mature *mumukṣutva,* a value for keeping in mind as one's primary goal *tattva-jñāna,* which is synonymous with liberation, *mokṣa.*

Adhyātma-Jñāna-Nityatvam

Adhyātma-jñāna-nityatva, the nineteenth value in the order told by Lord Kṛṣṇa to Arjuna, is discussed as the final value for the sake of more logical analysis.

The previously discussed value, *tattva-jñānārtha-darśana,* a value for not losing sight of the knowledge of truth as one's primary goal, is an attitude which, for its fulfilment, requires the gain of appropriate knowledge. How does one gain this appropriate knowledge, the knowledge of truth, *tattva-jñāna,* which is also the same as the knowledge of self, *ātma-jñana*?

Knowledge is not gained by sitting under a *bodhi* tree. Sitting quietly under a *bodhi* tree may be fine for some other things. Perhaps a reflective person sitting under a tree for some time may figure out certain things about the world and its miseries, but knowledge will not come to that person simply because he sits quietly. For any knowledge to be discovered, there must be a valid, effective and an appropriate means available to know whatever that one seeks to know. *Adhyātma-jñāna-nityatva,* deals with the valid, effective and appropriate means for gaining self-knowledge, *ātma-jñāna* which alone fulfils the value previously discussed, '*tattva-jñānārtha-darśana*', a desire for liberation which has matured into inquiry into *tattva*, the truth.

Adhyātma means centred on *ātman*, self, and *jñāna* is knowledge; *adhyātma-jñāna* is the knowledge for which the subject matter is *ātman*, oneself; *nityatva* indicates constancy. *Adhyātma-jñāna-nityatva* is constancy in knowledge centred on the self. Where can one find the teaching for which the subject matter is oneself, *ātman*? Not in the usual disciplines of learning, such as in mathematics, physics, or chemistry or in anatomy, physiology or psychology. Self-knowledge is the subject matter of a tradition of teaching called *Upaniṣad* or Vedanta or any name equivalent to these names. The scriptures, at the end of the Vedas, where this teaching is found, are also called by the name of the teaching, *Upaniṣad*. Thus, *adhyātma-jñāna*, the self-knowledge, indicates the teaching and the books containing the teaching whose subject matter is the truth of oneself, of the world and of the Lord are called *Upaniṣads*. In fact, the very word '*Upaniṣad*,'[2] etymologically, means *adhyātma-jñāna*.

So, *adhyātma-jñāna-nityatva*, centred on the knowledge of the self, is a value for constancy in the study of the scriptures known as the *Upaniṣad*s and other texts of Vedanta. *Nityatva* means constancy in scriptural study until self-knowledge is gained, clear and free from doubt. For the gain of any knowledge, the answer to the question, "How long must I study?" has to be, "Until you know it", which means "Until you understand the subject matter." The gain of understanding is not something for which a specific time can be set.

[2] The word '*upaniṣad*' is derived from the root '*sad*' whose meaning is 'to disintegrate', 'to destroy' and 'to reach'. The root has two prefixes, '*upa*' and '*ni*'. *Upa* means near. The self, *ātman* is not even the nearest; it is oneself. By the prefix '*upa*', *ātman* is implied here. About this *ātman*, there is ignorance and confusion. The prefix '*ni*' stands for very well ascertained knowledge, free from vagueness and error. '*Upa*' and '*ni*' together refer to *brahma-vidyā*, knowledge of *ātman* being Brahman. So, *brahma-vidyā* wears out the whole host of evils, *anarthas* that is cause of a life of becoming, *saṁsāra*. Positively this knowledge makes one recognise that one is *pūrṇaṁ brahma*. The word '*upaniṣad*' thus, tells 'what it is' and also 'what does it do'.

Gain of knowledge is not like gain of a result produced by an action wherein, given the relevant factors, the amount of time needed to produce a result by a particular act can be calculated based on experience. For example, in cooking one can closely calculate how long it will take to cook rice at a given temperature, at a particular pressure, using a particular cooking method. But the time for understanding cannot be similarly calculated. All that can be said for understanding is that if one wants to gain certain knowledge, using the proper means for gaining that knowledge, one must study until the subject matter becomes absolutely clear. If the knowledge you seek is that of calculus, it will not, of course, do you much good to study art or history, just because you find it easier. Such a choice would be like trying to see a rose through your ear because your hearing is sharp and your eyesight is dim. The right means of knowledge must be ascertained and used. However, when you have the right means of knowledge for the knowledge you seek, it is simply a matter of continuing to use that means until the knowledge is gained and is clear and steady.

The Gain of Knowledge: Listening, Reflection, Contemplation

The study of Vedanta, until knowledge of self is clear and steady, involves three things, listening, *śravaṇa,* reflection, *manana,* and contemplation, *nididhyāsana.* These are the three things that constitute constancy centred on self-knowledge, *adhyātma-jñāna-nityatva.* Of these, *śravaṇa* is the primary means; reflection and contemplation are concurrent but secondary means, being simply aids to *śravaṇa.* The basic *śravaṇa* is listening to the words and sentences of Vedanta unfolded by a competent teacher, but *śravaṇa* also can be the 'hearing' that occurs when one, by oneself, studies the written scriptures. *Śravaṇa* is study of Vedanta in order to find out what it has to say about oneself, about the world and about God.

Vedanta unfolds what Lord Kṛṣṇa calls *jñeya,* that which is to be known, that ultimate knowledge which is liberation itself. The ultimate *jñeya* of Vedanta is stated cryptically in the *mahā-vākya*s, great statements. These statements occur in the form of dialogues between the teacher and student in which the teacher unfolds the meaning of the *vākya*s by a teaching methodology, which makes precise, in context, the intent of each word. When unfolded, the *mahā-vākya* reveals the vision, purport, *tātparya,* of Vedanta. *Śravaṇa* includes a thorough inquiry into the meaning of these statements. Study of the great statement '*tattvamasi* - that you are', for example, requires an inquiry asking questions: Is this just a mystic statement to be enjoyed like a fanciful poem? Is it a factual statement? What is the meaning that Vedanta gives to this statement? Can one find out from Vedanta what is meant by 'that'? What is 'you'? What is the connection between 'that' and 'you'? What, if anything, does it mean to me right at this moment that I am a 'you', which is 'that'?

The answers to these and similar questions are found by studying the *mahā-vākya*s and other supporting sentences that unfold the great statements. The way of study is to listen to a teacher who is both a *śrotriya,* one who is learned both in the language of the *śāstra* and in the methodology of teaching and a *brahma-niṣṭha,* one who is clear and steady in the vision of the truth of himself. Such a teacher, by clearly creating a context for the student, will unfold the meaning of Vedanta word-by-word, sentence-by-sentence, negating the unintended meanings. The teacher will unfold not only the meanings of the words and sentences but also how the sentence connects to the previous sentence and how it is connected to the following sentence. The whole teaching of Vedanta is in the form of words; therefore, one must necessarily see what the words used are meant to unfold. One must see neither more nor less but exactly what the words are meant to unfold.

Using the words of Vedanta to 'see' myself is like using my eyes to see colour. If with my eyes open and focused I find that there is not enough light to see colour or to see it clearly, the light should be brighter. But the need for more light does not mean that it is the light that sees. The eyes remain the instrument that does the seeing. Similarly, words and sentences, like the eyes, are the means of seeing. To use these means, I must throw light upon the words and sentences, analyse them, and discover their exact meaning as unfolded by the scripture. These words are about me. With a fresh, open mind made ready by right attitudes, I try to discover what the words say about me. In order to discover, I question the words and sentences.

What do the words say about how I am connected to this world? How am I connected to the Lord if there is one? Is there a Lord? And, if so, is the Lord the creator of the world? What is said about this world? I must be related to the world someway. Am I inside the world as part of it? Or, am I just here, and the world is here, too, but each of us is independent of the other? Is the world created? If so, is that creator a person or a principle? In *śravaṇa* such questions are addressed to the words of Vedanta dealing with the individual, the world and the Lord, *jīva, jagat* and Īśvara.

Vedanta is studied to answer questions on each of these topics. In the beginning of study, these three topics are seen as a triangle with each topic enjoying its own identity, occupying its own position. As the study progresses, as the words and sentences of Vedanta are analysed in order to understand the nature of each of these entities, the 'triangle' disappears. The three are seen as one. You discover that the individual, the world and the Lord, *jīva, jagat* and Īśvara have their being in one thing, one absolute non-dual reality, and that reality you are, *tvamasi*.

THE VISION OF VEDANTA IS ONESELF

'You are That' is the vision of Vedanta. The entire Vedanta is about the self, about 'me', about what I am. In order to understand the scripture, I must clearly understand and keep in mind its basic topic, its basic vision. When the *śāstra* talks about the world, it is talking about me. When it talks about other worlds, heavens and hells, to which I may go, it talks about me. The purpose of Vedanta is not to throw light upon means and ends but to illumine the truth of all means and ends.

The first part of the Vedas, known as the *karma-kāṇḍa,* the part relating to actions, throws light on various means and ends. It is in the *karma-kāṇḍa* that I can discover the means for going to heaven, how to perform a ritual to bring rain or gain the birth of a son. If ends such as these are what I am interested in, the first part of the Vedas, namely the *karma-kāṇḍa* is the place to seek information. The last section of Vedas, known as Vedanta or *jñāna-kāṇḍa,* the section relating to knowledge, does not deal with the achievement of unachieved results. Vedanta talks about what I am, what the world is, what God means, what

God's nature is, and how God is identical with me. Vedanta involves no means and ends. It just throws light upon what is. Throwing light upon what is, is called knowledge. Knowledge is just seeing what is. Vedanta lights up the fact. Whether Vedanta talks about the world or God or about the deities or any other subject, all discussions only throw light upon one basic fact, that there is no difference between the individual, the world and God. This non-dual fact of the identity of God, the world and me is *tattva*, the basic, irreducible truth of everything. It is this *tattva*, which is unfolded by the teaching of Vedanta.

THE WORDS OF VEDANTA: APPROACH WITH CONFIDENCE

How does Vedanta reveal the truth? Through words. Words and sentences are the means of knowledge for the truth of everything that includes me. For knowing myself, words are the instruments, the means, even as my eyes are the means for seeing a rose. Therefore, my whole approach to using the words of Vedanta must be similar to my use of my senses. Consider how confidently I use my eyes. When I open my eyes to look at an object, I have complete confidence that I will be able to see whether the object is there or not. I do not doubt my ability to see the object or its absence; nor do I doubt the ability of my other senses to do their jobs. If someone asks me, " Do you have any honey in your cupboard?" I go to my cupboard with great confidence in my ability to find out whether or not honey is to be found there. What is the source of my confidence? The source of my confidence is my expectation that my sense organs can do their job properly. I have my eyes and if they are not very sharp, I have my nose. If my nose is not enough, I have my tongue and the sense of touch also. If I see a likely jar and put my finger in it, I can say, "Oh, this stuff must be honey." If I put my sticky hand to my nose, I will be more convinced, "I think it is honey." Then if I touch my tongue with my fingers, I can conclude, "Aah! Definitely honey." From where do I get the confidence to declare, "This is honey"?

I have confidence because I know that my sense organs work. I see, I smell, I touch and taste it. I know that it is honey. This is *pratyakṣa-jñāna,* knowledge obtained by direct perception through the senses. I come to the use of my senses with *śraddhā,* with faith or confidence in their ability to uncover for me perceptual knowledge of the objects they apprehend.

I need to come to the words of Vedanta with the same confidence with which I open my eyes, alert my ears, touch with my fingers, sniff with my nose, taste with my tongue, in order to discover the existence of a thing that is available for perception; with just such confidence I should open my mind to the words of Vedanta and see the facts these words reveal.

VEDANTA, THE PRAMĀṆA FOR NON-NEGATABLE KNOWLEDGE

The words of Vedanta are as much a means of knowledge, *pramāṇa,* as are my sense organs. In fact the knowledge given to me by my sense organs, upon analysis, can be dismissed, whereas, the knowledge I gain from the words of Vedanta cannot be dismissed by any other means of knowledge. Sense organs can reveal to me only the existence of things that are capable of being perceived, but what can be perceived by one means of perception or at one level, intensity or power, of a given means of perception can be dismissed by other perceptual means or at other perceptual level of capability of the same means.

What is perceived can always be dismissed. Upon sufficient examination nothing perceivable is, as it appears to be but always is, resolvable into something else. The perceived blueness of the sky is not really blue. The perceived daily ascent of the sun in the eastern sky does not really happen. Upon inquiry the perceived flatness of the earth can be dismissed. However, the words of Vedanta give a knowledge that cannot be dismissed. The knowledge unfolded by Vedanta, that there is one non-dual reality, cannot be dismissed by perception or by any perception-based logic, for all logic ultimately is traced back to a perception-base. Neither by perception nor by logic can the fact of non-duality be dismissed. This is how perception and logic play a role in the teaching and study of Vedanta. Although perception and logic may not reveal non-duality, they can never dismiss non-duality; they do not have the capacity.

Thus, *śruti,* which is heard, is an independent means of knowledge that commands from us, a respectful attitude toward the *pramāṇa,* the means, the words of Vedanta, which is even greater than the respect held for our eyes or other senses. This is true because the senses, unlike Vedanta, can deceive. The knowledge brought by my senses, is never absolutely true but, upon further analysis, is always subject to dismissal.

Previously we saw, in the introduction to the discussion of these values, that experience is not knowledge; that experience does not invariably confirm and much less does it reveal truth. Truth is gained through knowledge; only a *pramāṇa*, a means of knowledge can reveal truth. Further inquiry causes us to see that the means of knowledge, ordinarily at our disposal, are not adequate to reveal truth. The means of knowledge available to us, in our body-mind assemblage, are only perceptual means that can reveal certain useful, functional truths, the kind of useful information needed for daily life, but through which we cannot discover the *tattva*, the fundamental truth that we seek.

The blind man's elephant

The facts that our senses reveal is like the truth the blind men gained after each of them felt only one part of an elephant. In this traditional story, several blind men came upon an elephant, an animal none of them had encountered before. For a few minutes before the elephant's keeper took it away, each of the blind men was able to touch or grasp some portion of the elephant; and each was convinced that he knew what an elephant is like. They argued vigorously amongst themselves. One, who had put his arms around one of the huge legs, said, "An elephant, I know very well from my personal experience, is like a pillar." Another, who had laid his hands flat against the elephant's vast side, said, "No! It is like a wall." The others had different claims. "An elephant is like a rope," said the one who had grasped the tail. "Idiots! You are all deluded. An elephant is like a sharp pointed spear," implored the one who had touched a sharp tusk. The blind men each, confidently, claimed knowledge on the basis of having touched one part of the animal. In what each said, there was some truth in the untruth; and the untruth was connected to the truth. Thus, the knowledge each had was an untruth containing an incomplete truth, connected to truth. Further inquiry into each of the false truth by the mistaken blind men would lead to recognition that it was untruth or, at best, incomplete truth.

In fact, every untruth is always in some sense connected to the truth, although, perhaps, not in such an obvious sense as a leg or trunk is connected to the elephant. There is truth when an untruth is known as untruth; in this sense every untruth is connected to truth. In another sense there is a connection because the very status of untruth is dependent upon some truth, a fact that the untruth contradicts or does not completely, or adequately reflect the truth. For example, in the classic Vedanta illustration of the rope-snake in which a coil of rope mistakenly is thought to be a snake, an inquiry into the nature of the snake will reveal the rope; the rope, being the truth of the snake.

Thus, in the study of Vedanta, *śravaṇa* includes the analysis of untruth in order that, with the recognition of the untruth as untruth, the proper kind of inquiry can be undertaken to reveal the truth. The truths—sense organ data and logical conclusions based on sense data—gathered through the use of one's ordinary means of knowledge are no different from the blind men's elephant-truths; at best such truths are only functional, negatable facts, immediately useful but subject to contradiction by other truths and by the complete truth.

The truths of various philosophies, psychologies, religions and other belief systems also fall under the heading 'elephant-truth', that is, they offer some truth contained in untruth, or untruth connected to truth. The elephant-truth of the other means of knowledge and of the philosophies is contradicted by what is said in Vedanta. Just as the fact of the complete elephant contradicts the incomplete, wrongly identified truths of its parts, so does the absolute truth of 'what is' contradicts both the negatable truths of the *pramāṇa*s that reveal objectifiable reality, and the conclusions of philosophies based on incomplete truth or untruth. Vedanta contradicts the truth of one's senses and the conclusions of widely accepted belief systems, philosophies and psychologies; but what Vedanta says, cannot be contradicted by anyone. Vedanta is not contradictable.

Śraddhā : Suspension of Judgement Pending Discovery

All means of knowledge, *pramāṇas*, require suspension of judgement pending discovery, *śraddhā,* in their ability to deliver what is expected of them in order that one may do whatever is necessary to use the *pramāṇa*. Eyes are the means of knowledge for seeing. To see, one must engage one's mind behind the eyes, open the eye-lids, turn one's head in the right direction and do whatever else that is necessary, perhaps, turn on the light or put on eyeglasses, whatever may be called for under the circumstances. A person who knows himself to be blind would not be motivated to try to engage his mind behind his eyes or to turn on the light. But a person who has *śraddhā* that his eyes can see will be able to surrender his mind to his eyes, take whatever other steps that may be necessary, in order that his eyes may do their job. Similarly, with *śraddhā* one must surrender to Vedanta in order that it may perform its function as a *pramāṇa* for knowing oneself. Since Vedanta seems to contradict all one's usual means of knowledge, one must approach it with greater *śraddhā* than that accorded to one's senses.

However, *śraddhā* is not blind belief; it is suspending the judgement pending discovery. I must come to the words of Vedanta ready to have my old ideas contradicted, prepared to grant Vedanta the same latitude that I would give to a wise and respected friend who contradicted some observation of mine. Seeing something on the ground, I took it to be a snake and I cried out, "Be careful! There is a snake." But my friend calmly replied, "No, no! That is only a rope." I would not reject my friend's statement. Instead, for the time being I would suspend my judgement about what I had seen, blink my eyes, and look again. I would be willing to accept a contradiction to my prior conclusion. I would again check out what my eyes had to report and then say, "Well, you are right. It is a rope." With this type of faith one must approach Vedanta, with an attitude which holds in abeyance old notions and prejudices for the time being, judgements about oneself, the world and the Lord, allowing one to approach the words of Vedanta with a fresh mind.

ŚRAVAṆA IS THE PRIME MEANS OF KNOWLEDGE, REFLECTION AND CONTEMPLATION ARE AIDS

Hearing the great statements, *mahā-vākya*s, of Vedanta, is the primary means to gain the knowledge of oneself, *ātma-jñāna*. The *mahā-vākya*s are wielded as a means of knowledge by a teacher, in accordance with the teaching methodology, *saṁpradāya* of Vedanta, in which a context is created to expound the meaning of the words of the teaching. The listening or *śravaṇa* includes inquiry into and analysis of the meaning of the sentences in order to arrive at clear, ascertained knowledge of precisely what the sentences say. Concurrent with listening, but secondary to listening and listening-associated inquiry, are reflection, *manana,* and contemplation, *nididhyāsana.* It is through listening alone that knowledge is gained; but, as needed, reflection and contemplation are aids to listening. Even though we listen and the meaning of what is being heard is understood, the questioning intellect may raise doubts or, habit-born obstacles may cloud the understanding. Valid knowledge must be definite and clear. If doubts, vagueness or interfering habits of thought are present, reflection and contemplation will help.

Reflection is the use of reasoning to eliminate the doubts raised by the intellect challenging the self-knowledge gained through Vedanta. In terms of knowledge the intellect has a definite role to play because it is the faculty that assimilates and accepts knowledge. With its own presumptions, its own inferences, its own certain derivative forms of knowledge, the intellect poses questions to any knowledge that is gathered.

Thus, it is the job of the intellect, through the use of logic, to make the knowledge gained through Vedanta free from any possible doubt put forth by other means of knowledge.

The knowledge that has been heard, unfolded by Vedanta, is the non-dual oneness. The Lord and the individual are one. The Lord and I are one. I am limitless, but my perception contradicts what has been heard. Vedanta says there is one but what I see is many. My perception stands against the knowledge unfolded by Vedanta; and my reasoning, based on perceptual data, deals only with duality. So, what can the intellect do when confronted with the knowledge of Vedanta, the fact of non-duality? It can use its duality-based logic to establish the fallacy of duality. The ordinary perceptual means of knowledge cannot reveal non-duality but the knowledge of duality revealed by these means can be negated by the reasoning intellect itself. In reflection, *manana,* the doubts that arise because of perceived duality are eliminated by analysis that reveals the fallacy in the thinking process that poses the doubt. Reason, inescapably perception-based, cannot reveal non-duality but, with its own logic, it can establish that it cannot establish duality. Through reason's negation of duality the doubts challenging the knowledge of non-duality are removed.

The enquiry and analysis of *manana* also examine and dismiss the contentions of the various schools of thought that object to the knowledge of Vedanta. Many of the various philosophical systems and schools of thought pitted against Vedanta have been propounded by sharp wits; the major contenders against Vedanta are armed with logic. It is for the sake of one's own clarity that these schools must be dismissed, the fallacies in their contentions seen, the defects in their logic revealed by logic, all questions answered, all shades of meaning analysed. So, in reflection, one looks at all possible questions and answers them, both the questions of one's own inquiring intellect and the arguments raised by contending schools of thought. One answers the questions until the intellect can no longer raise any objections, because knowledge does not brook any doubt. There is no co-existence between knowledge and doubt, between knowledge and vagueness. Just as one throws gold into the fire so that it will come out even purer than before, one puts one's knowledge to the test of all questioning and doubts, one's own and the systematic arguments raised by others, so that it will come out more shining than before, shining more brilliantly each time it is unfolded by Vedanta. The knowledge shines, untouched by anything, unpolluted by any doubt, just as the object of knowledge, the self, is unattached, *asaṅga*, to anything.

It is the function of reflection, *manana*, to free the very process of thinking. Free thinking, thinking that is not stifled or chained, prepares one for the discovery of one's essential freedom by clearing away, through use of logic, all obstructive fallacies entertained by the intellect. It is through free thinking of reflection that any distortion of reason introduced by charismatic conditioning can be recognised and eliminated. Leaders, dead or living, of various schools of thought, of various belief systems, often gain great following. It must be seen that both ideas and beliefs followed by large number of people for a long period of time can be wrong. Neither the size of its following nor the length of the time entertained, establishes the truth of an idea or a belief. A large following, for a long time, does not establish knowledge; only a valid *pramāṇa* establishes knowledge. Knowledge, not the conclusions or beliefs advocated by some charismatic personality, is the subject matter of Vedanta. If we mix up personality and the subject matter of knowledge, both are spoiled.

LISTENING AND REFLECTION DISMISS DOUBTS CONTEMPLATION WEAKENS HABITUAL THINKING

Śravaṇa and *manana* account for the elimination of all one's doubts on Vedanta. *Śravaṇa* eliminates the doubts regarding Vedanta as means of knowledge. *Manana* eliminates the doubts about which is correct; knowledge from Vedanta or data from some other means or source. With all doubts removed, the intellect no longer poses a problem. The knowledge, 'That you are', 'I am Brahman, I am limitless' is accepted by the intellect. When the intellect does not pose a problem, what problem can there be? There can be one remaining problem; something called habitual thinking that can interfere with what is known. Habitual thinking is a repetitive thought process which, although, may have had some logic behind it initially, has become fixed as a habit, no longer linked to logic. A habit of thought is not logical, it just happens; like a mood, one just gets into it.

The kind of habitual thinking, which is a problem for knowledge, is sometimes called *viparīta-bhāvanā*, which means an opposite attitude. *Viparīta-bhāvanā* is an attitude opposite to the fact revealed by the knowledge of Vedanta, an attitude reflected by habitual thinking such as, 'There is security for me in these things. There is happiness for me in this situation.'

A wise person of great dispassion, *vairāgin*, with well-assimilated values requires only, *śravaṇa*, listening to Vedanta, for clear, steady knowledge; or, if some doubt is there, *manana* finishes the doubt. Afterwards, nothing more is required for knowledge to be firm and clear. But for whom dispassion is not so well established, notwithstanding *śravaṇa* and *manana* there may be some problem with habitual thinking. When habit-born thoughts oppose the fact of oneself—the knowledge of Vedanta—contemplation, *nididhyāsana* is useful. To eliminate habitual opposite thinking, contemplate. Contemplate on what you know to be the fact of yourself. See the fact that you are fullness that knows no lack. The more familiar one becomes with the fact of oneself, the less will there be the opposite attitude.

Nothing new is gained from contemplation. It is from listening, *śravaṇa,* the meaning unfolded of the words of Vedanta, that the knowledge of oneself is gained. Contemplation, like reflection, is an aid to *śravaṇa*. Listening is the means for knowing; reflection frees the knowledge from doubts; contemplation eliminates the habitual erroneous notions that obstruct the knowledge. The erroneous notions of opposite thinking are habitual rather than conclusive. Before listening and reflection, such notions were conclusive. Prior to the knowledge of myself, my conclusion was, 'I am the body. Various things in the world, apart from me, make me secure, bring me happiness'. After knowledge, such notions are no longer conclusive. After knowledge I know that I, limitlessness, am the only secure thing. I know that I, the non-dual reality of creator, creation and individual, am time-free existence, form-free awareness, absolute fullness that knows neither gain nor loss. However, even though weakened by knowledge, some of the old thinking, born of habit, may continue. Until such habitual thinking goes, the knowledge gained remains knowledge with certain obstructions. Knowledge may be there but stifled by obstructions; the fruit of knowledge is not enjoyed.

What causes the old thought habits to go? It is by seeing the fact of myself. The more I see myself the less will be the hold of old thought processes. Continued *śravaṇa*, listening, to the fact of myself unfolded by the teacher, helps me become more familiar with seeing myself. In addition, in contemplation, I highlight what I have seen and heard. The meaning of certain words, that tell the truth of my nature, which I have come to know through hearing, in contemplation I try to see the meaning without any thinking process. With the help of a word or a sound, I just try to see the fact of what I have heard. This simple seeing is called contemplation, *nididhyāsana*.

Thus, it is by these three means, listening, reflection, and contemplation, that one commits oneself to the pursuit of the value, '*adhyātma-jñāna-nityatva*', the value for constancy in the knowledge centred on self, which simply means constancy in the study of Vedanta. With the analysis of *adhyātma-jñāna-nityatva*, the individual examination of each of the twenty *jñāna*, value,is complete.

Values: Preparation For Listening, Reflection And Contemplation

Lord Kṛṣṇa called self-knowledge *jñeya,* that which is to be known because in the knowledge of the truth of oneself, released from all false sense of limitation, one discovers that one is the completely free being that one longs to be. Self-knowledge is liberation; and *śravaṇa,* listening, is the primary means for the gain of self-knowledge. For some, *śravaṇa* may be all that is necessary; but for others *manana,* and *nididhyāsana* are needed to make *śravaṇa* fruitful. So the three, listening, reflection, and contemplation, together, are the sole, primary means to self-knowledge. Of these three, listening is the principal, independent means and reflection and contemplation are aids to and dependent upon listening.

The values, which make the mind ready for listening, reflection and contemplation, are a secondary but necessary means for the gain of self-knowledge. The values are secondary in the sense that gain of the values alone does not bring about self-knowledge, but are necessary because without the assimilation, in some measure, of the values, the primary means, listening, aided by reflection and contemplation, will not work. Values are secondary to the gain of knowledge like fuel is secondary to the cooking of food. Fire or heat is the primary means for cooking food; but fuel or some energy source, although secondary to fire, is necessary in order to enable the fire to cook. Fire alone cooks, but there can be no effective fire without fuel. Through listening alone, which includes reflection and contemplation as needed, we gain self-knowledge; but there can be no effective listening in a mind not blessed, in relative measure, with the values. From *amānitva, adambhitva* through *adhyātma-jñana-nityatva,* and *tattva-jñānārtha-darśana,* the values are necessary making the mind ready for *śravaṇa*. Therefore, to be prepared to be a student of Vedanta, we need to discover within us, in some measure, a personal value for the twenty values or attitudes.

Understanding is the key to making the twenty values our own personal values. Attitudes that are accepted because they have been imposed as advice, counsel, admonition or obligation are not personal values but are restraint or conditioning. Such imposed obligatory values do not make the mind ready for self-knowledge. Only personal, assimilated values establish the mental climate for *śravaṇa*. The values become personal when we see the value of the value to us very clearly. When we clearly see the value of a value to us, that value becomes our personal value. However, even after the values become personal, for sometime, we may have to be very alert with regard to the particular attitude; otherwise, habit will continue to rule. Moreover, once we understand that there is a value for a value, thereby making it a personal value, then after a period of alertness, when we deliberately take whatever actions will make the value more real to us, the value will become assimilated.

An assimilated value is very natural. Spontaneously, it is part of us. With alertness all our personal values become our assimilated values, a natural part of us that, without effort or control, express themselves spontaneously in our life. When in relative measure this happens, when we see the value of value to us and, to some extent, have assimilated these attitudes, our mind is ready for *śravaṇa-manana-nididhyāsana,* hearing-reflection-contemplation, through which we gain the knowledge of the self, that ultimate *jñeya,* that which is to be known, which reveals the truth of the self to be time-free, form-free, full and complete existence, awareness, that knows no want, no limitation, no isolation.

EPILOGUE - THE DAILY VALUE OF VALUES

The attitudes and ways of thinking called *jñāna*, values, are specified for students of Vedanta but are relevant to everyone. Reflecting a keen insight and a profound grasp of the working of the mind, the mental stances described as preparation for Vedanta comprise a mind that is a beautiful, objective instrument, quiet, alert, effective, ready for any study or pursuit. Such a mind, not split by internal conflict, undismayed by external adversity, has the best possible preparation for daily life as well as for the study of Vedanta.

Values enhance the quality of life, whatever our activities may be. Our daily life gains efficiency and cheerfulness, even radiance, when these values are personal, assimilated norms. We become cheerful persons, both saintly and effective. Generally, we consider a saintly person non-effective. The benevolence and accommodation that characterise a saint are seen as accompanied by a lack of efficiency in worldly matters. It is not so. True saintliness makes one the most effective person possible in any situation or transaction. It is because such a person can be totally objective. His or her appreciation of given circumstances is not clouded by subjective conditioning; there is neither need for self-validation through a particular interpretation of facts nor for self-fulfilment through a desired outcome. A saint clearly sees facts for what they are and can make and act upon a fact-based judgement free from subjective interpretation or need. A person not affected by the situation is the person effective in the situation.

Thus, although the primary purpose of *jñāna,* values, as told by Lord Kṛṣṇa to Arjuna, is to prepare the mind for self-knowledge, when the total value of these values is understood, one sees that these attitudes have the highest personal value for everyone. The *jñāna,* values impartially bless and make more effective both the mind of the everyday struggler and of the sincere seeker. The everyday struggler seeks fullness in the pursuit of *artha,* securities and *kāma,* pleasures, whereas the mind of the *mumukṣu–jijñāsu,* the seeker of knowledge for the sake of liberation who, having discerned the futility of limited ends and means, seeks fullness through the gain of self-knowledge, through the study of Vedanta.

Oṁ tat sat

For a list of our other publications, please visit the website at:
www.avrpt.com

...or contact :

ARSHA VIDYA RESEARCH
AND PUBLICATION TRUST
32 / 4 Sir Desika Road,
Mylapore Chennai 600 004
Ph : 044 - 2499 7131
Email : avrandpt@gmail.com
Website : www.avrpt.com

ARSHA VIDYA GURUKULAM
Anaikatti P.O.
Coimbatore 641 108
Ph : 0422 - 2657001
Fax : 0422 - 2657002
Email : office@arshavidya.in
Website : www.arshavidya.in

SWAMI DAYANANDA ASHRAM
Purani Jhadi, P.B.No. 30
Rishikesh, Uttaranchal 249 201
Telefax : 0135 - 2430769
Email : ashrambookstore@yahoo.com
Website : www.dayananda.org

ARSHA VIDYA GURUKULAM
P.O. Box 1059. Pennsylvania
PA 18353, USA
Ph : 001 - 570 - 992 - 2339
Email : avp@epix.net
Website : www.arshavidya.org

Our publications are also available at all leading bookstores and downloadable through the 'Teachings of Swami Dayananda' APP for Android and Apple devices.

SWAMI Dayananda

PASSED AWAY IN
2016

known as a philanthropist

TAttavidamanda = Jenna's teacher